BIG
DUMMIES
OF THE
BIBLE

STEPHEN M. MILLER

W PUBLISHING GROUP™

www.wpublishinggroup.com

A Division of Thomas Nelson, Inc.
www.ThomasNelson.com

Published by W Publishing Group, a Division of Thomas Nelson, Inc., P.O. Box 141000, Nashville, TN 37214.

W Publishing Group books may be purchased in bulk for educational, business, fund-raising, or sales promotional use. For information, please e-mail SpecialMarkets@ThomasNelson.com.

All Scripture quotations, unless otherwise indicated, are taken from The Holy Bible, New Century Version, copyright © 1987, 1988, 1991 by W Publishing Group, a division of Thomas Nelson, Inc. Used by permission.

Other Scripture references are from the following sources:

The New King James Version (NKJV), copyright © 1979, 1980, 1982, Thomas Nelson, Inc., Publishers.

The Holy Bible, New Living Translation (NLT), copyright © 1996. Used by permission of Tyndale House Publishers, Inc., Wheaton, Illinois 60189. All rights reserved.

Cover Design: Tobias' Outerwear for Books

Author is represented by the literary agency of Alive Communications, Inc., 7680 Goddard Street, Suite 200, Colorado Springs, CO 80920.

Library of Congress Cataloging-in-Publication Data

Miller, Stephen M., 1952–
  Big dummies of the Bible: and how you can avoid being a dummy too / Stephen M. Miller.
    p. cm.
  Summary: "Mistakes made by men and women in the Bible, how we are still making the same mistakes now, and what to do to avoid the inevitable pain and heartache"—Provided by publisher.

  ISBN 0-8499-0770-5 (tradepaper)

1. Christian life. 2. Bible—Biography. 3. Errors. 4. Fallibility. I. Title.
  BV4501.3.M548   2005
  220.9'2—dc22   2005008089

Printed in the United States of America
05 06 07 08 09 RRD 9 8 7 6 5 4 3 2 1

Contents

INTRODUCTION

Glanced yet at the list of big dummies?

If so, I know what you're thinking.

Solomon?

Yep, I'm afraid he's in here.

I know the Bible calls him the wisest person in human history—then or ever. But who said wisdom is any match for stupidity?

It's not.

Stupidity doesn't play by wisdom's rules. Even the smartest people sometimes do the dumbest things. Enter Solomon with his thousand wives and their baggage, which includes idols.

Let me make one thing as clear as I can. No one in this book is a complete idiot.

Some of the people—like Solomon and his father, David—are incredibly smart. Others—like Esau who traded his inheritance for a bowl of soup—leave us wondering if they passed their free time by head-butting goats.

But whether they are wise or common senseless, these people have given us some of the Bible's most engaging case studies of dumbness. Their stories are worth reading for two reasons. For one thing, it's reassuring to know there are people dumber than we are. And for another, we human beings learn from mistakes—whether it's our own mistakes or the mistakes of someone else. We experience misery—vicariously or in the flesh—and we're suddenly wiser.

Pain is funny that way. It makes us want to go in a different direction.

That's the point of this book: to learn from the mistakes of others.

I know it's tempting to make fun of these people and leave it there. Some of the dumb things they did are entertainingly stupid. Samson tells Delilah three lies about how to sap his strength, and every time she gives it a try. Finally he tells her the truth: he has never had a haircut. Then he takes a nap with his head on her lap, and he expects to wake up with hair.

That's delicious. It's hard to imagine someone that dumb.

Until I look in the mirror.

Much as we'd like to deny it, the more we think about these big dummies of the Bible, the more we can see ourselves in them. It doesn't take much to become a big dummy—just one incredibly ridiculous mistake. That'll do.

Fact is, I could entertain you quite nicely with some of mine. But I'd just as soon let someone else do it—about two thousand years after I'm dead.

In the meantime, I'm learning from my mistakes. And I hope you're learning from yours. But I think we can both learn from mistakes of big dummies of the Bible.

A word of thanks to:
- Linda, my wife, frontline proofreader, perpetual supporter, and constructive critic.
- Rebecca and Bradley, our children, also known in various

circles as Becca and B-Rad, both of whom counsel me on my projects and charge a slight fee.

- Chip MacGregor, my agent, who wears a kilt on special occasions. He can't throw a Scottish hammer very far, but he sure can pitch a book idea.
- Greg Daniel, my editor with two first names, who loved the book but felt it needed a better title; he was right, of course.

God bless them, every one.

And God bless you as you read this book and, more importantly, as you read his Book.

—Steve

1
ADAM
AND EVE

God gave this couple only one law to obey,
but it was one law too many.

Humanity's first couple made just one dumb decision, as far as the Bible says. But it was a paradise show-stopper.

No other dumb decision in human history can match it for the trouble it caused. In fact, the Bible in a nutshell is the story of God working his plan to undo the damage.

"You may eat the fruit from any tree in the garden," God had told Adam and Eve, who were basking in Eden's perfect glory. "But you must not eat the fruit from the tree which gives the knowledge of good and evil. If you ever eat fruit from that tree, you will die!" (Genesis 2:16–17). There you have it—before the Ten Commandments there was only one, and this was it.

As it turns out, it was one commandment too many.

A SIN TO CHEW ON

Creation's story is full of mystery. There are many more questions than answers. And one of a landslide of questions is why God didn't want Adam and Eve eating fruit that gives the knowledge of good and evil. Scholars don't know, but they love to guess.

One theory is that "good and evil" represents wisdom that comes with maturity, which prepares us for independence and our emerging sexual awareness. Adam and Eve were like children who weren't ready for any of that. In time, God would have let them eat the fruit of that tree, but this wasn't the time. They weren't ready. In the same way that eight-year-old girls shouldn't be having babies and eight-year-old boys shouldn't be driving Saabs down the boulevard, Adam and Eve had no right eating the forbidden fruit. That's one theory.

For whatever reason God prohibited the fruit, humanity's first couple got duped into eating it. A talking snake—identified in Revelation 20:2 as the devil—assured Eve, "You will not die. God knows that if you eat the fruit from that tree, you will learn about good and evil and you will be like God!" (Genesis 3:4–5).

Eve took a long, hard look at the fruit. It certainly seemed like it would be tasty. So she ate some, and then she gave some to Adam, who also ate it.

Insight of some sort poured into them, because they suddenly realized they were naked. So they made themselves some clothes out of leaves.

It's too bad most of us don't read Hebrew, the original language of the Old Testament. We miss a lot of subtle symbolism and some entertaining wordplay. Readers in ancient times might have laughed out loud at the wordplay here. Adam and Eve wanted to get as smart as God—they desired to be "shrewd" but they ended up "nude." From smarty pants to no pants at all.

Some of us have nightmares like that. We're standing front and center before a crowd of lofty dignitaries in a place of great honor, only to discover to our horror that we're as naked as a plucked jaybird. If we're lucky we have a briefcase, because we know how to use it.

Adam and Eve had fig leaves—nearly footlong fans that were among the largest tree leaves in the Middle East. In God's eyes, though, they were overdressed because wearing anything at all meant they had more to hide than body parts.

Learning from Adam and Eve's Mistake

Knowing When to Say No

As a father of teenagers, I know many of my children's teenage friends quite well, some of them for years. When one of those boys stopped dating a girl he had been seeing for several weeks, I asked him why.

The boy, a sixteen-year-old Christian, paused. I imagine he was trying to decide whether or not to tell me. Finally he said, "She doesn't have any boundaries."

"How so?" I asked.

He said that when they were sitting alone together at her house, watching TV, she took the arm he rested on her shoulder and pulled it down, placing his hand on her breast. He said he pulled his hand away and put it in his pocket.

The young man said he broke off the dating because he didn't think the relationship could be the same after that. He didn't think he could handle the temptation, knowing that she was OK with that level of intimacy.

I was stunned. When I was a kid, most of the boys I knew considered hand on breast as a goal, not a foul.

Had this teenage boy been Adam, I can't imagine him biting into the forbidden fruit. This boy, it seems to me, is one solid piece of evidence that God's plan to reclaim creation and overpower sin is actually working.

GOOD-BYE EDEN, GOOD-BYE GOD

"The Fall" is what many call the sin of Adam and Eve. Their world collapsed.

Some politicians and high-profile business execs caught in scandals manage to ruin their careers, dishonor their families, and devastate their health. But they produce only a tiny ripple in a pond compared to the Kilimanjaro-high tidal wave that Adam and Eve unleashed on the planet.

In the beginning, God created. Sometime thereafter, Adam and Eve redecorated. What they did, however, was no more an improvement than slicing a tattoo into the flesh of God's finest masterpiece or spray-painting graffiti onto the towering walls of the Grand Canyon. Adam and Eve not only uglied up their own lives, but they uglied up the entire world.

The Sin That Damaged Creation
Theories don't get very far in trying to make sense of how the sin of Adam and Eve changed God's good creation for the worse and how their sinful tendency seems to pass along so effectively from one generation to the next—perpetuating the damage.

Perhaps there's something genetic about this "original sin" or "sinful nature," some theologians have speculated. Others declare this is nonsense, arguing that if the problem is physical, we'll some-day be able to fix it ourselves. But it's a spiritual problem, they insist, that intrudes into the physical world, and that only God can fix.

This much is clear: the utopian world that the Bible says existed before the feast on forbidden fruit is nothing like the harsh world described afterward—the world we know. And whether or not Adam and Eve passed along some mystical sin nature that connects us to their original sin, we've each sinned on our own. Plenty.

The Bible's main storyline is about God working to restore his good creation and to defeat sin. He washed the sinful world with a flood, saving the family of one righteous man, Noah. From Noah's ancestors, God chose righteous Abraham to become father of a nation devoted to him—a nation intended to serve as a model of goodness to the rest of the world. From that nation came his own son, Jesus, "who takes away the sin of the world"—at least for those who believe in him (John 1:29; 16:8–9). In the end, God promises, we will see "a new heaven and a new earth. . . . God's presence is with people, and he will live with them, and they will be his people . . . and there will be no more death, sadness, crying, or pain, because all the old ways are gone" (Revelation 21:1, 3–4).

Just as God once walked with Adam and Eve in a paradise, the time is coming when he will walk with his people again—creation restored, sin and its painful side effects gone.

Booted from Eden

Before deporting Adam and Eve from the Eden paradise, God arranged for the couple to trade in their fig leaves for clothes he made from animal skins. This is the first time the Bible speaks of animals dying because of the sins of humans—perhaps a predecessor of animal sacrifices yet to come.

"The man has become like one of us," God said. "He knows good and evil. We must keep him from eating some of the fruit from the tree of life, or he will live forever" (Genesis 3:22). Adam and Eve had apparently been allowed to eat fruit from this tree—until now. But to keep them from living forever, "The LORD God forced the man out of the garden of Eden to work the ground from which he was taken" (v. 23).

Losing Their Relationship with God

Worse than losing Eden, Adam and Eve lose God.

Nowhere else in Israel's ancient story preserved in the Bible does anyone seek Eden on a quest for the perfect place to live. But throughout Israel's history, God's people never stopped seeking him. They sought him at the national worship center. They searched for guidance from him through prophets, priests, and sacred writings. They called on him in prayer.

Even today, God's people still seek him. But now they do it with a promise from his son, Jesus: "Search, and you will find. Knock, and the door will open for you" (Matthew 7:7). Relationship restored. Next up: walking in paradise. Before walking in paradise, however, we must live with the resulting consequences of the first couple's sin.

Women's Sentence

God imposes the consequences that the couple brought on themselves, starting with Eve. "I will cause you to have much trouble when you are pregnant, and when you give birth to children, you will have great pain. You will greatly desire your husband, but he will rule over you" (Genesis 3:16).

The word translated "pain" is a rare one in the Bible, and it seems to mean more than physical pain. Other words from the same root are often translated as worry, agony, and grief. Even in our modern world of drug-laced, high-tech medical care, pregnancy is all of that—along with physical pain.

God's added sentence that women will be ruled by their husbands is debated hotly enough to bake bricks that you could throw later. Some argue that women should obey their husbands, much like a slave obeys a master. "Just do it."

But in the context of childbirth, God's provision for continuing the species after death enters the landscape, others argue that male dominance refers to a woman's desire to have children. This powerful desire puts her in a position to be dominated by her husband, who may not share the same compelling desire for a family.

But this wasn't God's original plan—the plan that got distorted by sin. God created Eve as Adam's "helper" (Genesis 2:18). The Hebrew word also means partner or companion. It's a word used to describe God: "Our hope is in the LORD. He is our help, our shield to protect us" (Psalm 33:20).

Eve was no more a gofer for Adam than God was for Israel. They worked together in a healthy relationship until sin got in the way.

Learning from Adam and Eve's Mistake

Mr. and Mrs. Who's Boss?

When I was in a young adult Sunday school class back in my college days, I remember one particular class session. A young married woman with one of the best singing voices in the church began to cry. She said she believed the Bible was telling her to let her husband be lord of the house. And this lord didn't like her going to church. I saw her much less after that day.

My mom, however, was a different bird. After she got saved in the Pilgrim Holiness Church, she told Dad that God would always be first in her life but that Dad would be right there in second place. "I can live with that," Dad said.

But Dad didn't like Mom's going to church every Sunday. Some Sundays, Mom and the four small kids she had at the time (another came later) walked about a mile to church, even in the Northeastern Ohio winter. She didn't have her Ohio driver's license yet, and Dad thought that by refusing to drive her to church she wouldn't go. Dad still had a few things to learn about Mom.

The Bible's teaching about husband-wife relationships gets argued a lot—sometimes with loud voices. Some readers say that wives should defer to their husbands. Others say that advice like that was more culturally appropriate for ancient patriarchal times, when men were the leaders and women weren't even allowed to own property.

God made man and woman partners, to help each other. Yet in Paul's famous advice to husbands and wives, he tells women to submit to their husbands and he tells husbands to love their wives. All of his advice, however, follows this introduction: "Submit to one another out of reverence for Christ" (Ephesians 5:21 NLT).

The lord of the house is the Lord.

Men's Sentence

"You listened to what your wife said, and you ate fruit from the tree from which I commanded you not to eat," God told Adam. "So I will put a curse on the ground, and you will have to work very hard for your food" (Genesis 3:17).

Farmers know all too well that thorns and weeds grow much better than most crops. You almost have to coax up a crop, against its better judgment. But weeds need no encouragement. They come to watch the coaxing and to entertain themselves by strangling the crops when farmers' backs are turned.

Return to the Dust

"You must not eat the fruit from the tree which gives the knowledge of good and evil. If you ever eat fruit from that tree, you will die!" (Genesis 2:17).

Some scholars say God wasn't talking about physical death, since Adam lived to the ripe old age of 930. They argue that God was talking about spiritual death—separation from God, a bit like the isolation that King Saul later experienced after God rejected him. Prophet Samuel refused to meet with Saul anymore. As far as Samuel was concerned, Saul was dead (1 Samuel 15:35).

Most scholars, however, see physical death in God's threat, and certainly in the sentence that God later imposed on Adam and Eve: "You will return to the ground, because you were taken from it. You are dust, and when you die, you will return to the dust" (Genesis 3:19).

It's quite possible, these scholars say, that God intended humanity to live forever, enjoying fruit from the tree of life. But sin changed all that. The apostle Paul later wrote, "Sin came into the world because of what one man did, and with sin came death. This is why everyone must die—because everyone sinned" (Romans 5:12).

But God began working his plan. "As one sin of Adam brought the punishment of death to all people, one good act that Christ did makes all people right with God. And that brings true life for all" (v. 18).

What's "true life"? Jesus makes this as obvious as a hunk of fruit dangling from a tree never again forbidden: "Whoever hears what I say and believes in the One who sent me has eternal life" (John 5:24).

Adam and Eve made the dumbest mistake in human history. But it's nothing God can't fix.

Learning from Adam and Eve's Mistake

Living Forever

Many scholars say we have Adam and Eve to thank for one of the most troubling mysteries of all: what happens to us when we die? We owe that mystery to them, the scholars say, because humans were made to last. We weren't supposed to die. The sin of Adam and Eve changed that.

Sin, however, doesn't get the last word; God does. God is restoring his damaged creation. He gave us incredible proof with the resurrection of Jesus. There is life after death.

That's not the only evidence.

Many of us who have lost loved ones experience an innate sense of assurance that they live on. And some people who have been with the dying tell of near-death experiences that seem to be yet another kind of assurance from God.

On hand to witness one such spectacle was Dr. Paul Brand, renowned surgeon, leprosy specialist, and coauthor of *Fearfully and Wonderfully Made* and *In His Image*. His patient and friend Rose Kato lay tied to the railings of her hospital bed. She would be dead in a few hours from an infection, but for the moment she was fighting to break loose. Dr. Brand arrived with his wife, and he ordered the restraints removed and the tubes taken from Rose's mouth so she could talk.

She sat up and beamed. "Isn't it wonderful! Can't you see him?"

"Rose, who should I be seeing?"

"It's Jesus! He's come for me! There he is! Can't you see him? He's standing at the end of the bed just waiting for me! And you people are trying to hold me back!"

Dr. Brand and his wife wept. "We just embraced her and assured her that Jesus had come for her and that she would be seeing him soon, in Glory. . . . She died that night in great peace."

Did Rose *really* see Jesus?

"I have no doubt," Brand said.

God's people were built to last, and with God's loving help, they do.

No Question Is a Dumb Question

1. Bible experts can only guess about why God didn't want Adam and Eve to eat the forbidden fruit. Some think the couple wasn't mature enough and that God would have let them eat it when they were ready. What do you think?

2. Adam and Eve knew it was wrong to eat the fruit, but they did it anyhow. Humans ever since have been doing the same: they know something is wrong, but they do it anyhow. Why do you think people do that? Did the sin of Adam and Eve somehow reprogram humanity, tilting them so they lean into sin? If so, how do some people manage to get reprogrammed, so they lean toward God and goodness?

3. If you could talk to the boy in the feature "Knowing When to Say No," what would you say to him? What would you say to the girl? From what you know about Christian teenagers today, whose action better reflects the typical Christian: the boy or the girl? Do you agree that the boy's response is one piece of evidence that God's plan to reclaim creation and overpower sin is working?

4. One of the fallouts of the Fall is that women became dominated by men. Is that adequate reason for a husband to impose his will on a wife and to insist that he's the leader of the household? Or is that fallout's connection to sin a reason to do the opposite and to treat a wife as an equal? Paul advised husbands and wives to submit to each other (Ephesians 5:21). At what point does submission have to end—when a man or a woman has to put a foot down?

5. "Living Forever" talks about people having an innate sense of immortality. Do you have a sense at the level of your instincts that assures you that you're built to live forever? What about the story of Dr. Paul Brand's dying friend, who had a deathbed vision of Jesus? What do you think of stories like that?

Adam and Eve Recap

DUMB DECISION	ROTTEN RESULTS
Don't eat the fruit from one tree in the world—that's the only restriction God gives Adam and Eve. They eat the fruit anyhow	• Their sin somehow damages creation. • They get booted from Eden. • Women are sentenced to painful childbirth and domination by their husbands. • Men are sentenced to a lifetime of hard labor. • Humans are destined to return to the dust from which they came.

2
DAVID

He ruled Israel like a lion,
but he ruled the roost Like a ruptured duck.

In macho Bible times when men were men and everyone else was something pitifully less, one of the Bible's most pathetic scenes is of a man crying for his wife.

Crying wasn't the worst of it. He tagged along behind her like an abandoned, whimpering puppy as she walked to the home of her new husband: King David, already married to at least six other women.

The woman with the weepy husband apparently didn't want to go any more than her husband wanted her to go. But David insisted.

It was the first of several incredibly stupid family decisions David made, decisions that produced hatred, rape, rebellion, and murder—all in the family.

He ruled the Middle East like a lion, but he ruled the roost like a ruptured duck.

We expected more of Israel's greatest king:

• Shepherd boy whom God handpicked to lead Israel because David had a heart like God's own

- Brave young man who killed lions and bears to protect his flock and then protected his nation by defeating in mortal combat a Philistine giant whom no Israelite soldier had the courage to face

- Gifted musician whose velvet hum of the harp calmed his troubled king

- Insightful poet who wrote psalms so enduring that the faithful still recite them three thousand years later

- Cunning warrior who not only tamed the Philistines who had bullied the Israelites for centuries, but who defeated all of Israel's neighboring enemies, securing the borders

- Savvy politician who united a loose-knit coalition of family tribes into a Middle Eastern superpower that no one wanted to provoke

This was the man—Israel's most revered king in a thousand years of kings—who with a wave of his sword introduced the Jewish nation to their one and only golden age of prosperity, power, and prestige.

Kingdom glorious but family notorious.

How Not to Woo a Woman

The woman David ordered home was his ex-wife: Princess Michal, one of King Saul's daughters.

She had loved him once and even helped him escape assassins whom her insanely jealous father sent to their home. As far as Saul was concerned, a king shouldn't have to stand in the shadow of someone else's fame—even the fame of a giant-killer son-in-law. Michal delayed the assassins long enough for David to slip out of the house and run away to begin his new life as fugitive—a shepherd on the lam.

Michal began a new life, too, though probably not of her own choosing. In this macho man's age, fathers decided whom their daughters would marry. Saul had given her to David in exchange for the foreskins of one hundred Philistines—a price Saul hoped David wouldn't be able to pay but would die trying. Now, with David on the run—and dead if he came back—Saul annulled the marriage and gave Michal to another man: Palti, son of Laish.

During the several years that passed, David built an army in the southland—and a family. While making his headquarters in Hebron, a day's walk south of Jerusalem, he married six women: Ahinoam, Abigail, Maacha, Haggith, Abital, and Eglah (2 Samuel 3:2–5).

Life moved on for Michal too. Though the Bible stops short of saying she fell in love with her new husband, the rest of her story makes it seem a sure bet.

Saul and most of his sons died in a battle with the Philistines. Saul's commander survived and offered to help make David the new king. David agreed on one condition: "Give me my wife Michal. She was promised to me, and I killed a hundred Philistines to get her" (v. 14). Bought and paid for, she was his legal property.

Why David insisted on breaking up an apparently loving family to add a seventh wife to his harem remains a mystery. Perhaps he still loved her, in his manly man way. More likely, Bible experts say, it was a matter of politics and not the heart. As Saul's daughter, Michal provided legitimacy for David's claim to the throne. We see it today in countries that have kings and queens; we expect someone in the royal family to inherit the throne. But it seems odd that David would care about that, since his authority to rule came from God. "Appoint him," God had told the prophet Samuel as young David approached, "because he is the one" (1 Samuel 16:12).

Michal left for David's home in Hebron, at the command of

her brother, weak-willed Ishbosheth, Israel's king for a moment. Saul's military commander, Abner, apparently convinced Ishbosheth it was the right thing to do, though it was really just part of Abner's plot to give the nation to David.

As Michal began the daylong walk to Hebron from her village just north of Jerusalem, Palti went along, "crying as he followed" (2 Samuel 3:16). He walked all the way to his tribal border. He may have gone the rest of the way, too, but Abner ordered, "Go back home!" Palti obeyed, and the Bible never mentions him again.

Michal surfaces just one more time, several years later. David was king, and he was dancing in the crowded streets of Jerusalem. Not just dancing politely but "with all his might" (2 Samuel 6:14). He was part of a jubilant procession escorting Israel's most sacred object: the ark of the covenant, a chest holding the Ten Commandments. Michal looked out of the palace window and saw David's less-than-regal dance. She was disgusted. When David got home, Michal dished him up a full plate of sarcasm: "With what honor the king of Israel acted today!" (v. 20).

Her story ends with this bitter note: "Michal, the daughter of Saul, remained childless throughout her life" (v. 23 NLT).

Happily married, David was not.

Learning from David's Mistake
Forcing Ourselves on Others

We all hate rejection. We want people to like us, agree with us, and back us up no matter what. When they don't, we can get frustrated, angry, and even cruel—especially if we're in a position of authority over them. All we're asking for is loyalty. That's what we tell ourselves and them, but it's a lie. What we really want is to control them, to tell them what to think, what to do, and how high to jump.

Even God doesn't ask that much. He gives each of us the right to make up our own mind, think what we want, and reject him if we choose. He gives us that much freedom because he knows that it's useless to impose himself on us—worse than useless, it's repelling.

That's why Jesus gave this advice to his disciples when he sent them on a preaching tour: "If the people in a certain place refuse to welcome you or listen to you, leave that place" (Mark 6:11).

When we give people the freedom to disagree with us, we're keeping the door open. In time they may change their minds, or we may discover that they were right all along.

BATHSHEBA, THE ORIGINAL BATHING BEAUTY

By that springtime afternoon when the very married King David saw the very married Bathsheba in the flesh—and nothing but—he was already sire of a huge family. The Bible names only seven of his wives at the time and sixteen of his sons. But it adds that after moving to Jerusalem, where he saw Bathsheba, "David took for himself more slave women and wives. . . . More sons and daughters were born" (2 Samuel 5:13).

Where David found the time, energy, and libido to do what he did with Bathsheba is a screaming tribute to stupidity's power to knock down all obstacles. Not a lineup of beautiful wives, a herd of noisy kids, a nation of problems to solve, or even a war raging a three-day march from the palace door would keep King David from a naked lady.

It probably all started innocently enough. In the late afternoon, David took a stroll on the palace roof. Flat-topped, most building roofs served much like our decks and porches do today as a place to relax or do light chores in the open air. David probably wasn't looking for trouble, but he got an eyeful.

Bathsheba likely wasn't trying to turn up the heat. She probably didn't fling off her clothes and push her bathtub out to the front yard for the entertainment of her neighbors. Many houses in Middle Eastern cities were built around open-air courtyards, with walls on all four sides. But from David's perch on the palace roof, he saw what Bathsheba's neighbors couldn't.

He liked the view; he decided to get a closer look.

After finding out that the bathing beauty was the wife of Uriah—one of his soldiers on the battlefront, fighting for king and country—he invited her to his place.

No one knows if Bathsheba was as dumb as David and willingly agreed to his request for an encore undressing. Perhaps what she heard was the order for a command performance from the Alpha Male. For whatever reason, she and David did what the Song of Solomon—a book, ironically, named after their son—only talks about.

Stupidity layered on stupidity, David took these incredible risks for the lust of his umpteenth woman:

- **The death penalty.** For at least two centuries, a basic Jewish law ordered: "If a man has sexual relations with his neighbor's wife, both the man and the woman are guilty of adultery and must be put to death" (Leviticus 20:10).

- **His reputation.** David had a flock of wives, while Uriah had just the one, lone lamb. This affair was so brazenly selfish that if leaked, spin control wouldn't fix it. David's reputation would be forever slimed, and he would wind up in books about big dummies of the Bible.

- **His DNA.** If it wasn't just any bath that Bathsheba took—if it was the required ritual purification one week after her menstrual flow stopped—she was as fertile as fertile gets.

Bathsheba got pregnant. Away at war, Uriah would have been the dumbest of all to have believed he was the father.

Learning from David's Mistake
What to Do When You See a Naked Lady

If you're a man and she's not your wife, there's just one word of advice. The Bible gives it over and over in stories and sermons: run away.

An Egyptian official's wife tried to seduce young and handsome Joseph. When she slipped off his cloak, he "ran out of the house" (Genesis 39:12).

Paul told Christians in the promiscuous seaport town of Corinth to "run away from sexual sin" (1 Corinthians 6:18).

Life-savvy elders advised young men to stay away from any married woman trying to seduce them: "Don't even go near the door of her house" (Proverbs 5:8).

Job planned ahead: "I made an agreement with my eyes not to look with desire at a girl" (Job 31:1).

Men are wired to look. But they can be wired to recognize trouble when they see it too. It's one dumb ox that follows a bovine beauty into the butcher shop.

A Bathing Beauty Cover-Up

David had a bright idea, though a little late. He ordered Uriah back to Jerusalem and asked him how the war was going. After the chat, David told Uriah to go home and get some rest—expecting Bathsheba to give her husband a warm welcome. But Uriah slept just outside the palace door.

"Why didn't you go home?" a stunned David asked the next morning.

"The soldiers of Israel and Judah are staying in tents . . . ," Uriah answered. "It isn't right for me to go home to eat and drink and have sexual relations with my wife!" (2 Samuel 11:11).

David's bright idea number two was to get Uriah drunk that night and try again. As long as Uriah got home—even if nothing happened—Bathsheba could convince him that he was simply too drunk to remember their lovely evening together.

It didn't work. Even drunk, Uriah was more honorable than Israel's greatest king.

David's bright idea number three was to die for. He had Uriah deliver his own death sentence—in a sealed message for the commanding general. "Put Uriah on the front lines where the fighting is worst and leave him there alone. Let him be killed in battle" (v. 15). Uriah died in a spray of arrows, and Bathsheba cried when she got the news.

After the customary period of mourning, typically a week, she joined David's harem. Women couldn't own property, so widows without sons were instantly destitute. Citizens watching from a distance must have thought it big of their king.

Prophet Nathan knew better, and he said so. Though David immediately repented, Nathan warned that the consequences were unstoppable. Quoting God, Nathan said, "I am bringing trouble to you from your own family" (2 Samuel 12:11).

The baby boy died. And David's family troubles were just beginning.

No Way to Treat a Princess

David's oldest son, Amnon, first in line to be the next king, fell in lust with his half sister, Tamar. Pretending to be sick, he convinced David to send the virgin princess to his room to feed him. Then he raped her.

By law, a rapist had to give money to the victim's father and then "marry the girl, because he has dishonored her, and he may never divorce her for as long as he lives" (Deuteronomy 22:29). In that macho culture, raped women were often considered damaged goods that no one wanted.

But Amnon kicked her out of his house. This sent two loud messages:

- As crown prince, he was above the law.
- Tamar wasn't even fit to marry a rapist.

When David heard the news, he got mad at his son—but said nothing. Tamar left what was probably a guarded residence inside the palace, reserved for the king's daughters. She moved in with her full brother, Absalom. Witnessing her despair each day must have tormented Absalom. It probably humiliated him, too, that Amnon thought he could get by with treating Absalom's sister like discarded trash and that Absalom was too weak to do anything about it.

Two years later, Absalom invited his big brother to a sheep-shearing festival. There, he got Amnon drunk, assassinated him, and then ran for his life to the homeland of his maternal grand-parents, in what is now Syria, near the Sea of Galilee.

David eventually got over Amnon's death, but he couldn't stop missing Absalom, the new crown prince. After three years, David's nephew and military commander, Joab, convinced the depressed king to invite Absalom home. Yet when the prince came back, David refused to see him—for another two years.

By the time the two finally reunited, Absalom was so bitter that he decided to launch a coup. Popular among the common people, Absalom succeeded in running David out of Jerusalem. Absalom might well have won the war if he hadn't relied on the advice of a counselor who secretly supported David. Instead of quickly attacking David's retreating forces, Absalom agreed to delay and further build his army. But this bought David time to do the same.

In the battle that came later in a forest, Absalom ran into some of David's troops. He tried to get away on his mule, but the thick branches of an oak tree snagged his long hair, jerked him off the mule, and dangled him in midair like a bull's-eye. David had given orders to spare Absalom, but commander Joab thought he knew what was best. "Joab took three spears and stabbed him in the heart" (2 Samuel 18:14).

When David got the news he wept, "My son Absalom, my son Absalom! I wish I had died and not you" (v. 33).

David had no one to blame but himself. His dumb decisions killed his two oldest sons. Israel's most admired king, a giant-killing superhero in the eyes of many, was just another flawed family man who couldn't discipline his wandering eyes or his wavering sons. So his family paid the price.

Learning from David's Mistake
When It's Time to Speak Up

For most of us, a cork in the mouth would improve our lives and probably make the world a better place. We tend to shoot off at the mouth first and gather the facts later—if we can recognize them all shot to pieces.

There are times, however, when speaking up is the toughest thing in the world. That's because, for a change, we actually think about the problem before saying anything. And we come to the conclusion that if we say what we think, we're going to get in trouble or we're going to hurt someone we love.

God stands for justice, and so do his people. When it's within our power to do the right thing and we do nothing, we help no one and we hurt everyone—including the person we think we're protecting. King David thought he was protecting his rapist son, but in the end it was David's silence that killed the prince.

No Question Is a Dumb Question

1. Like David, many leaders even today suffer with what seems to be more than their fair share of family troubles. That includes world leaders, top business executives, even pastors. What's the problem?

2. David forced his ex-wife, Michal, to leave her new husband and come back to him. Why do you think he felt justified? If he really wanted to express his love to Michal and get her back, what do you think would have been a smarter approach? What effect does it have on you when someone forces you to do something you don't want to do?

3. David took incredible risks in his affair with Bathsheba. Why would he risk so much? And why do people today still take those kinds of risks? Of the four pieces of advice from the Bible that the author mentions in the feature "What to Do When You See a Naked Lady," which one do you like best, and why? If men are wired to look at beautiful women, can they be rewired to recognize trouble when they see it?

4. David didn't punish his rapist son, Amnon. What do you think he should have done? How could punishing Amnon have turned David's family toward a brighter future?

5. The author says that David's silence is what killed Amnon and that we all need to speak up for justice. What justice issues do we need to speak up for today? How should we speak up? What difference do you think it would make?

David Recap

DUMB DECISIONS	ROTTEN RESULTS
He orders ex-wife Michal to leave.	She hates David and dies childless.
He Has affair with Bathsheba.	She gets pregnant.
He decides to cover up the affair by murdering Bathsheba's husband and marrying her.	He gets caught, and the child dies.
He refuses to punish his son, who raped a half sister.	The victim's full brother, Absalom, murders the rapist and flees the country.
He refuses to see Absalom after inviting him home.	Bitter, Absalom leads a coup against his dad.

3

ESAU

Except for one bowl of soup, the Jew's founding fathers could have been Abraham, Isaac, and Esau.

There are smart people in the Bible who made dumb decisions, and there's Esau. He was a bonehead. It's as simple as that. On rare occasions he stumbled across a smart decision, but they were rare and seem out of character.

The Bible paints him as a redneck. Figuratively and literally. "Born red . . . his skin was like a hairy robe" (Genesis 25:25). In fact, some people started calling him Red (*Edom* in Hebrew). What exactly was reddish, skin or hair, scholars aren't sure. For some redheads, it's both.

Either way, the Bible's description wasn't intended to compliment him. Redheads in ancient times were outcasts. Their distinguishing color wasn't particularly distinguishing. Even as late as the Middle Ages, ending in the 1400s, artists painted the betrayer of Jesus, Judas Iscariot, as a redhead.

Besides being red-skinned or red-haired, Esau was excessively hairy. Unfortunately for him, the follicle enhancement of any color—blond, brunette, or redhead—was considered uncouth, uncivilized, and lowbrow. A hairball baby like Esau—who must have looked like the son of Bigfoot—would have projected the crude image of a sorry slob even lower than lowbrow—perhaps no brow, no neck, and a belch that split wood.

According to Middle Eastern custom of the day, Esau should have become father of the Jews. After all, he was the oldest son of Isaac, from whom the Jews descended. But his younger brother, Jacob, outsmarted him—no major achievement.

LESS THAN IDENTICAL TWINS

Esau was the older of twin sons. He was born one body length ahead of Jacob, who was clutching Esau's heel at birth. That's how Jacob got his name, from the Hebrew word for "heel." And as far as Esau was concerned, Jacob lived up to his name; he was lower down than the heel on a centipede.

These twins were opposites in many ways. (See chart on facing page.)

Differences between these twins would eventually shatter the family unity and send Jacob packing to what is now Turkey on a desperate run for his life from Esau.

Like many family blowups, the trouble started small—over a bowl of beanlike lentil soup.

MY KINGDOM FOR A BOWL OF SOUP

"One day Jacob was boiling a pot of vegetable soup. Esau came in from hunting in the fields, weak from hunger" (Genesis 25:29).

If Esau was like many hunters today, he went out before day-break without breakfast. Some hunters seem to think that skipping the meal sharpens their senses, giving them a predator's edge over the prey. But all it did for Esau was sharpen his hunger pangs.

One of the big questions about what happened next is why the

ESAU	JACOB
• An outdoorsman who loved hunting and roaming the fields	• A stay-at-home son who preferred life in the camp
• So hairy that naked he looked more bear than bare	• Smooth-skinned
• Daddy's boy, perhaps partly because less-than-adventurous Isaac also seemed to be a connoisseur of the gourmet meat Esau bought home from hunting	• Mommy's boy, perhaps because they spent a lot of time together. But perhaps also because God told Rebekah before the birth that her younger son would rule the older one
• Lived in the moment and didn't give much thought to the future	• A schemer who set set careful goals and then pursued them relentlessly

son of a rich man was doing the cooking. Isaac had inherited the tremendous wealth of his father, Abraham. And Abraham had so many herds and servants that he had to part company with his nephew, Lot. Even the huge fields of Israel couldn't sustain them both.

Isaac's family certainly had servants who could have done the cooking—many servants.

For this reason, some wonder if Jacob was setting up his brother for the kill. If so, there's an irony at work: Esau the predator in the fields returned home to become the prey in the camp.

Perhaps Jacob had cooked these meals during many hunts before, anticipating Esau's return at roughly the same time. In this way, Jacob could have programmed Esau to expect hot food waiting for him. We can't be certain it happened like this, but the story doesn't read like a coincidence: famished hunter arrives home to the savory scent of stew wafting gently about the camp. There seems a bit of intent at work.

Jacob's soup of the day was a high-protein lentil stew, simmered in red sauce—for a brother who loved red and was Red.

"Let me eat some of that red soup," Esau said (Genesis 25:30). It's not hard to imagine Esau standing there with hairy hands cupping the biggest bowl in the camp, with his bearded jaw cranked open to reveal one of the few parts of his body without hair: his teeth.

"You must sell me your rights as the firstborn son," Jacob replied (v. 31).

That would qualify as price gouging. That's a bit like telling someone who lost his home in a tornado that he could have a room for the night if he signed over his retirement assets—mutual funds, IRAs, CDs, piggybank change, and his collection of John F. Kennedy half dollars.

Let's look at two of Esau's most important rights as a firstborn son in the ancient Middle East—rights that Jacob demanded.

Two-Thirds of Isaac's Wealth and Property
All younger sons got one share, but the oldest son got two shares. With just two sons, that meant two-thirds went to Esau and one-third went to Jacob. It's unclear if Jacob was asking Esau to give up both of his shares, which would have left Esau with nothing, or just the extra third that belonged to the oldest son. In that case, Esau would have held on to one-third of the inheritance—the third that belonged to Jacob.

Leadership of the Extended Family

The oldest son typically became leader of the clan, or extended family. That's all of the families and servants once led by the father. That meant Esau would have held legal authority even over his brother's household. Esau, for example, could have drafted Jacob's sons and servants to help fight off raiders.

"I am almost dead from hunger," Esau told his stew-stirring brother. "If I die, all of my father's wealth will not help me" (Genesis 25:32). So Esau sold his part of the family wealth to Jacob for what we can only hope was an incredibly tasty lentil soup.

In all of recovered history from the ancient Middle East chiseled onto stone slabs and cylinders, and scratched into pottery fragments, there's no human being on record who was dumb enough to sell his entire inheritance for anything, let alone for something as fleeting as a bowl of soup. There are examples of brothers selling some of their inherited property to one another, but at fair market price.

One bowl of soup, no matter how tasty, was not worth a single sheep in trade—and certainly not worth a expansive landscape covered in sheep and shepherds. Yet in the mind of Esau, which must have been located somewhere in his digestive tract, he was able to justify this expense.

Staggering stupidity is the only way to explain Esau's decision, based on the Bible's report: "Esau showed how little he cared about his rights as the firstborn son" (v. 34).

Who in his right mind would trade a wealth of inheritance for a bowl of soup? Someone driven by the desire of the moment, with no regard for long-term effects. Someone who didn't think ahead. Someone we'd love to play in a million-dollar chess championship.

Learning from Esau's Mistake
Me First

A young man I knew from church took off his wedding ring and put on a new ring he bought for himself.

He said the new ring symbolized the devotion he was going to start showing to himself for a change. Still in his early thirties, this man said that for too long he had been putting others first, especially his wife and kids, sacrificing his own important hopes and dreams.

Actually, he had started putting himself first several weeks earlier, when he began an affair with a married woman in the church. His new ring came after the other woman confessed their sin.

I know a little about sacrificing hopes and dreams for someone else, especially for my kids. My wife and I left a comfortable home in an affordable neighborhood and moved across town to one of the most affluent counties in the nation for one reason only: to get our kids out of a discouraging school system and into one of the best school districts in the area.

We traded in a house that was almost paid off for a house we'll never pay off. We gave up friends of twenty years in the old neighborhood. And we left behind the grandparents, my wife's mom and dad, who were suddenly almost an hour away instead of five minutes.

I struggled over this decision for weeks before committing to the move. In the end, this is the thought that released me: *I might be making a dumb decision, but my intention is to help my kids. And if I have to suffer to help my kids, that's OK. Whether I'm suffering or not, and whether I'm here or there, God will never leave me.*

I can understand the young man's desire for another woman—she certainly was lovely. But she was someone else's lovely. Another man's lovely wife. Another family's lovely mom. The young man ripped her away from all of them, as though he had not only a desire for her, but a right to her no matter who got hurt.

We have no idea how far the hurt reaches. The person who broke the news to me was a mutual friend. In all the years I have known her—pushing two decades—I've seen her cry only once. It was when she told me about this affair. I doubt the young man ever knew his actions had so deeply hurt this lady who was observing from a distance.

Selfishness to the complete disregard of others, as in Jacob's exploitation of his brother's stupidity, seems more than sinful. It looks like insanity, and perhaps it is. But it need be only temporary, thanks to God's grace—that divine characteristic willing to accept us where we are, but not willing to leave us there.

In time, brothers Jacob and Esau found forgiveness, as did the other woman, whose marriage survived. Even the young man, whose marriage failed, eventually rediscovered the God who had never left him.

We don't need to put ourselves first. We're always first with God.

STOLEN: DAD'S DYING WISH

Blind and frail, Isaac asked a favor of his older son: "I am old and don't know when I might die. So take your bow and arrows and go hunting in the field for an animal for me to eat. When you prepare the tasty food that I love, bring it to me, and I will eat. Then I will bless you before I die" (Genesis 27:2–4).

Even though it was common for elderly fathers to give their sons a blessing—a prayer that usually expressed hope for prosperity, health, and peace—Isaac's request is bizarre for a couple of reasons.

Jacob's Exclusion

It was common for fathers to bless their sons together, in a family ritual. Jacob would do that very thing a generation later, when he blessed his dozen sons gathered around his deathbed. But Isaac excluded Jacob for some reason.

Esau Sold His Rights

The first blessing belonged to the firstborn son, but Esau had traded away his firstborn rights. Either Isaac

- didn't know this,
- didn't feel bound by this agreement between his sons,
- didn't consider the honor of the firstborn as something that could be traded like property, or
- knew about the price gouging but wanted to teach Jacob a lesson in family values.

Whatever the reason, Esau should have seen Jacob coming, and coming with a plate of hot food.

Actually, the deception that followed was their mother's idea. Rebekah overheard Isaac's request and hatched the plot for Jacob. Perhaps her heart was in the right place, intending to help God fulfill his prophecy to her when she was pregnant: "Two nations are in your body. . . . The older will serve the younger" (Genesis 25:23). As if God needed the help of a sneak who would cheat a blind man out of his dying wish. Jacob certainly was his mother's boy.

The scheme: while Esau was out hunting, Rebekah would cook Isaac a goat-meat meal that Jacob would deliver, pretending to be Esau. Jacob would wear Esau's clothes, which would make him smell outdoorsy like his brother. And he would wear goatskin strapped to his hands and neck to make him feel more hairy than any human had a right to be.

To Jacob's credit, he protested the plan. To his shame, his protest mentioned nothing about the morality of cheating his father and brother. He was afraid of getting caught. "My brother Esau is a hairy man, and I am smooth! If my father touches me, he will know I am not Esau. Then he will not bless me but will place a curse on me because I tried to trick him" (Genesis 27:11–12).

"If your father puts a curse on you," Rebekah answered, "I will accept the blame. Just do what I said and go, get the goats for me" (v. 13).

Rebekah either didn't know what she was talking about, or she was lying. That much becomes clear after a quick look at what the Bible says about blessings and curses:

- Blessings and curses released spiritual power that made things happen, for better or worse. More than a simple prayer, in which people asked God for something, blessings and curses presumed God would do as requested. That's why when Moses and the Israelites had to pass through one particular nation on their exodus from Egypt to Israel, the king of that nation hired an internationally famous seer, Balaam, to curse the invaders. Instead, the seer blessed them three times.

- The words were irrevocable. Once spoken, the words couldn't be unspoken or rewound.

- They were nontransferable. Rebekah could no more take a curse spoken to her son than Esau could take a blessing spoken to his brother—even a blessing intended for Esau.

Jacob carried out his mother's plot with the skill of a seasoned con artist. There was just one problem. When Jacob opened his mouth, Esau didn't come out; Jacob did. The two didn't sound at all alike. Imagine Pee Wee Herman saying to a blind country music fan whose hearing is enhanced because of the blindness, "Hi, I'm Johnny Cash."

"Are you really my son Esau?" Isaac asked.

"I am," Jacob said.

Isaac touched Jacob's goatskin-covered hands and said, "Your voice sounds like Jacob's voice, but your hands are hairy like the hands of Esau" (Genesis 27:22).

Suspicious, Isaac ate the food and drank the wine, which would have dulled his senses a bit.

After the meal, the still-suspicious Isaac asked Jacob to come over and give him a kiss. Isaac took a quick whiff of Jacob's garments and smelled Esau's outdoor scent. Perhaps Isaac concluded that his eyesight wasn't the only sense eroded by aging; perhaps his hearing was playing tricks on him too.

So, finally convinced he was speaking to Esau, Isaac offered this blessing: "May God give you plenty of rain and good soil so that you will have plenty of grain and new wine. May nations serve you and peoples bow down to you. May you be master over your brothers, and may your mother's sons bow down to you. May everyone who curses you be cursed, and may everyone who blesses you be blessed" (vv. 28–29).

Learning from Esau's Mistake
Words We Can't Take Back

Isn't it intriguing that words come from breath, given the fact that once spoken they are as much alive as the breathing person who created them? It's a bit like we're all pregnant—men, women, children. And with each breath, we deliver a new life.

I don't find it strange that Old Testament blessings and curses were considered irrevocable. Everything anyone says is irrevocable. We can try to take it back, but all we can do is increase the word population.

Let's say that in a moment of frustration you tell your son that he's a disappointment to you. When you calm down and come to your senses, where are you going to find the rewind and erase buttons?

Or perhaps in an angry argument you tell your wife that you could have done better than her. Is there any word you can set loose like a snake-hunting mongoose to devour that sentence?

What about your parents? How many times do you have to tell them that they were good parents to you before those words will crowd out the swarm of others you spoke in years past?

It's no wonder that a sage in New Testament times offered this stark piece of advice: "always be willing to listen and slow to speak" (James 1:19). If we have to speak—and we probably don't have to nearly as much as we want to— we should choose our words carefully. We want to bring good words to life.

But try as we might, words best unspoken will some-times slip out. And once out, they're alive as long as the memory of the listener lasts. That's the bad news. Nothing we say can take the breath of life out of those words.

Still, there's hope for those of us with jaws quicker than our brains. "Love will cover a multitude of sins" (1 Peter 4:8, NKJV).

Words alone had no hope of healing the relationship between Jacob and Esau. Words alone are just as useless today. But words backed up with love can heal the deepest wound.

How do we love them?

"Let me count the ways. We love them to the depth and breadth and height our soul can reach."

And we pray to the good Lord that our voice doesn't carry that far.

BLESS ME, FATHER, FOR I HAVEN'T SINNED

A little while later, Esau delivered his gourmet meal to his freshly fed father.

"Who are you?" Isaac asked.

"I am your son—your firstborn son—Esau."

Old Isaac started shaking all over and asked, "Then who was it that hunted the animals and brought me food before you came? I ate it, and I blessed him, and it is too late now to take back my blessing" (Genesis 27:32–33).

Lions growl loud and low, and sopranos scream high C, but it takes a man robbed of his father's dying wish to produce the raging roar that exploded from Esau's lungs. After the roar came a plea.

"Bless me—me, too, my father!"

"Your brother came and tricked me. He has taken your blessing," Isaac answered.

"Jacob is the right name for him. He has tricked me these two times. He took away my share of everything you own, and now he has taken away my blessing." Then Esau asked, "Haven't you saved a blessing for me?"

"I gave Jacob the power to be master over you, and all his brothers will be his servants. And I kept him strong with grain and new wine. There is nothing left to give you, my son."

"Do you have only one blessing, Father? Bless me, too, Father!" Esau began sobbing, like a little boy who had just realized what his stupidity had cost him.

Isaac offered this measly blessing, which sounds more like a curse with only a weak trace of a blessing: "You will live far away from the best land, far from the rain. You will live by using your sword, and you will be a slave to your brother. But when you struggle, you will break free from him" (vv. 39–40).

So Jacob gets the good land and Esau gets the bad. Jacob gets plenty of rain to nourish crops and flocks; Esau gets dust. Jacob gets peace with other nations, Esau gets war. Jacob leads the family; Esau follows.

The best Esau can hope for is to cut himself free from Jacob, and he decides to do that sooner rather than later. "My father will soon die, and I will be sad for him. Then I will kill Jacob" (v. 41).

That was Jacob's clue to exit, stage north—about five hundred miles north. Only after spending twenty years in what is now Turkey, and raising a family of a dozen sons and a daughter, did Jacob come home to face Esau. In an uncharacteristically smart move, Esau met him with an army of four hundred men.

Both brothers, wealthy now, reconciled. Another smart move. They settled in different regions; Jacob moved into his former homeland of what is now Israel, and Esau lived in an arid region in what is now Jordan that eventually took his nickname: Edom.

Had their father gotten his dying wish, it would have been the other way around. And Jews today would be speaking of their founding fathers as Abraham, Isaac, and Esau. But God knew it wouldn't turn out like that. He knew Esau's dumbness would get in the way.

To what must have been Jacob's surprise, old Isaac was still alive. Rebekah, however, had died. Perhaps Jacob and his father reconciled too. When Isaac finally died, his twin sons reunited to bury him and then lived in peace with each other. Ten years later, the brothers parted one last time. Jacob and his family moved to Egypt's Nile River valley to escape a seven-year drought in Israel.

The two families spent close to half a millennium apart. Jacob's descendants, the Jews, stayed in Egypt for four hundred thirty years, eventually becoming a slave race until Moses freed them. When they came home, Esau's descendants, the Edomites, didn't trust them enough to let them pass through their territory.

NO QUESTION IS A DUMB QUESTION

1. What should Esau have done instead of selling his inheritance for a bowl of soup? What's one of the dumbest things you've ever seen anybody do? What were the consequences for the knucklehead? How did you or others who were witnessing it react? What would have been a smart alternative to the dumb deed?

2. After spending a few years on the planet, observing humanity, what have you noticed are some of the most common problems that drive relatives and friends away from each other, leaving them estranged for months, years, or even a lifetime?

3. Favoritism was a problem in Esau's family. Dad liked Esau best. Mom liked Jacob best. What kind of damage does this do to the individuals and to the family as a whole? What kind of favoritism have you seen in families today? What are some practical ways that parents can avoid showing favoritism among their children? Sometimes kids ask their parents, "Which one of us do you love most?" What do you think of this answer: "I love every one of you all the way to the top just like you love your dear old dad and mom"?

4. Do you think that when Jacob spent twenty years away from home that he thought much about what he had done to his brother and father? Some people say regret is a bad thing, and that it's harmful to dwell on it. Others say spending time thinking about regrets is a good thing because it shows we care enough about someone to be sorry for what we said or did, and teaches us what to do and not do.

What do you think? Is it a dumb idea to spend time thinking about regrets?

5.   Jacob sent gifts to begin his apology to Esau. What do you think is an effective way to ask forgiveness from a relative or a close friend?

Esau Recap

DUMB DECISIONS	ROTTEN RESULTS
Famished after a hunting trip, Esau buys a bowl of soup from his price-gouging brother, Jacob—paying for it with his future inheritance.	At the very least, the soup cost half of what Esau would have inherited from his rich father—and possibly everything.
When it comes time to receive his father's deathbed blessing—a prayer for prosperity—Esau doesn't warn him to watch out for Jacob's tricks.	Jacob steals the blessing, and Esau vows to kill him. This breaks the family apart; Jacob runs for his life and doesn't come back for twenty years.

4

HAMAN

Not quite Hitler,
his scheme for a massive holocaust
ended with him dangling from gallows built for a Jew.

Suicide by character flaw killed Haman.

He was the Persian Empire's prime minister, who was second in command only after the king, but Haman had two fatal flaws:

- His swollen ego enabled him to justify wiping out the entire Jewish race as punishment for one Jew's refusal to bow to him.
- His carelessness caused him to miss one crucial fact when plotting the holocaust: the king's wife was a Jew.

The day Haman discovered Queen Esther was Jewish became a day of added stature for him. But that's only because hanging by the neck until dead usually stretches a victim's spinal cord far enough to break it.

Celebrating Haman's death and a holocaust missed became the Jewish holiday of Purim—still observed in Mardi Gras–style every spring.

WHEN GOOD POSTURE IS OFFENSIVE

Haman was Iranian, by today's map. Most likely a wealthy noble, he lived in the Persian Empire's capital city of Susa. That's about one hundred miles north of the Persian Gulf, just across the border from what is now Iraq.

King Xerxes appointed Haman as his top official—a job a bit like prime minister. In recognition of Haman's elevated status, and at the king's command, people bowed when Haman walked by. At least most people did.

One man didn't: Mordecai, apparently a lower-level palace official. Day after day, as Haman walked by, Mordecai stood at attention. When other officials asked him why he didn't bow, he simply said he was a Jew. Eventually, the officials reported this to Haman, to see if Jews were exempt from bowing.

The next time Haman took a walk through the palace courtyard, he kept his eyes on Mordecai. When he realized the report was true, he decided that if Jews thought they were exempt from bowing because of Mordecai, he would personally see to it that they weren't exempt from dying because of him. He began plotting genocide on an imperial scale, covering all Persian-controlled lands from India in the distant east to Greece and Libya in the far west.

Why Mordecai didn't bow remains a mystery, because Jews typically did bow to kings and other royal officials. One possibility is that Mordecai considered Haman and his ancestors enemies of the Jews. Haman was an Agagite descended from King Agag of the Amalekites, the first people to attack Israelites during the Exodus. Fighting continued between the two races for centuries, until the Jews finally overpowered the Amalekites and ran them off.

Haman went to the king and said, "There is a certain group of people scattered among the other people in all the states of your kingdom. Their customs are different from those of all the other people, and they do not obey the king's laws. It is not right for you to allow them to continue living in your kingdom. If it pleases the king, let an order be given to destroy those people. Then I will pay seven hundred fifty thousand pounds of silver to those who do the king's business, and they will put it into the royal treasury" (Esther 3:8–9). That's three hundred seventy-five tons of silver—more than the empire's total annual income from taxes paid by all the conquered nations combined. Haman intended to confiscate Jewish property and apparently use part of it to pay the king's fee. In effect, Haman was buying a license to hunt Jews—a permit for a holocaust. Kill now, pay later.

Remarkably, the king agreed. He issued an irrevocable decree without even bothering to ask who this "certain group of people" was. For all he knew, he could have been married to one of them. And as it turned out, he was.

Confident of the king's reply, Haman had already selected a date to begin an ethnic cleansing intended to nourish his ego: by our calendar March 7, 473 BC, which was eleven months away. He selected the month and day by chance, throwing something called a "lot," or *pur* in Hebrew. That's where the Jewish holiday of Purim gets its name.

Messages translated in all languages of the empire were sent everywhere, announcing the date of the Great Jew Hunt and Property Grab. Jew killers would get to keep at least some of the wealth they looted, and probably all of the land.

Learning from Haman's Mistake
Us against Them

There are so many different kinds of human beings even in our own neighborhoods. It's tempting, and perhaps natural for organizer-types, to separate them by:

- color
- net worth
- language preference
- education
- religion

But that's just the first step. Next up is the rating system. And we all want our group to be among the valued. We don't want national leaders debating whether or not we deserve healthcare, top-flight education, or the right to live in this country as free and respected citizens. We want all of that. All of us do.

God wants it for us too. He doesn't want us to label one group as less valuable than another—us against them. He made all of us in his image and gave us some of his most important characteristics: the power to think, choose, love, and create. "Love your neighbor as you love yourself," Jesus said, (Matthew 19:19). That's hard to do when we think we're more important than our neighbor.

DEAD MAN WALKING

Mordecai immediately contacted Queen Esther, a cousin he had adopted and raised, and they began working on a strategy to protect the Jews and spring a deadly trap on Haman.

Somewhere in the middle of all that, the king had a tough time falling asleep one night. Perhaps knowing the sedating qualities of government documents, he started reading the daily palace journals. Though God isn't mentioned by name in the book of Esther, what happened next has convinced many that God is certainly implied—directing the drama. King Xerxes discovered that Mordecai once reported an assassination plot, and the king never rewarded him.

Haman had just finished building gallows seventy-five feet

high, and he came to the palace that evening to get the king's permission to hang Mordecai, the no-bow Jew. But the king spoke first: "What should be done for a man whom the king wants very much to honor?" (Esther 6:6).

As certain as he was stupid, Haman assumed the king was talking about him. "Have the servants bring a royal robe that the king himself has worn," Haman answered. "And also bring a horse with a royal crown on its head, a horse that the king himself has ridden. Let the robe and the horse be given to one of the king's most important men. Let the servants put the robe on the man the king wants to honor, and let them lead him on the horse through the city streets. As they are leading him, let them announce: 'This is what is done for the man whom the king wants to honor!'" (vv. 8–9).

The king loved this idea.

But it was Mordecai who rode the horse, as Haman walked in front—a servant—holding the reins and shouting to the crowds, "This is what is done for the man whom the king wants to honor!"

Learning from Haman's Mistake
Bragging Rights

Some of us are geniuses at self-promotion. We wear our title like a Medal of Honor that never leaves our chest. We buy the most stylish clothes, insisting that our position in society demands it. We accept nothing less than the best available seat in the house.

At a banquet one day, Jesus noticed a group of self-promoters trying to outdo each other. They were jostling for the seats of honor nearest the host. He saw a perfect opportunity to teach them a lesson.

When someone invites you to a wedding feast, don't take the most important seat, because someone more important than you may have been invited. The host, who invited both of you, will come to you and say, "Give this person your seat." Then you will be embarrassed and will have to move to the last place. So when you are invited, go sit in a seat that is not important. When the host comes to you, he may say, "Friend, move up here to a more important place." Then all the other guests will respect you. All who make themselves great will be made humble, but those who make themselves humble will be made great. (Luke 14:8–11).

You won't find a teaching like that in many books about success today. Yet the message rings true. The people we respect most are the people who treat us as equals and friends, the people who will give their choice seat to us and take a chair on the back row.

LAST SUPPER

Queen Esther risked execution by going to the king without an invitation. It was the same rule for everyone: uninvited guests could be killed. Fortunately, the king was delighted to see her and asked what had brought her to him.

Rather than tell him bluntly about her problem, she asked to spend some time with him first, promising to bring her request later. She invited him to a banquet and asked him to bring Haman. They all ate together that evening, and Esther convinced the gentlemen to join her the next night as well. It didn't take a hard sell, especially for Haman, floating somewhere in ego heaven, wallowing in the newfound attention of royalty.

Life was good and getting better. So thought the big dummy.

Sipping wine at the next day's banquet, the king asked what it was that Esther wanted.

"My people and I have been sold to be destroyed," she began, "to be killed and completely wiped out. If we had been sold as male and female slaves, I would have kept quiet, because that would not be enough of a problem to bother the king."

"Who has done such a thing?" the king asked.

"Our enemy and foe is this wicked Haman!" (Esther 7:4–6).

Livid, the king stormed out of the room—perhaps wondering what he could possibly do about his irrevocable decree ordering a holocaust.

Haman knew he had eaten his last supper unless he could convince Esther to save him. Pleading for his life in frenzied terror, he apparently fell on the couch where Esther was reclining during the meal. There was strict protocol in the palace about how to approach royalty, especially a queen from the king's harem. Falling on top of her was not a way to score points. Sadly for Haman, the king walked back in at that moment.

There are different ways to interpret what the king said, and one of them takes full advantage of Haman's position on top of the king's wife. Others are more general: "Will he even attack the queen while I am in the house?" the king declared (v. 8).

Oddly enough, given Haman's questionable position on the couch, it was a palace eunuch who offered a solution: "Look, a seventy-five foot platform stands near Haman's house. This is the one Haman had prepared for Mordecai, who gave the warning that saved the king."

"Hang Haman on it!" the king replied (v. 9).

With what reads like a chuckle, the narrator reports, "Then the king was not so angry anymore" (v. 10).

King Xerxes gave Mordecai the job Haman had just vacated. The king was powerless, however, to revoke his irrevocable Kill the Jews Day. But he could, and did, give Jews permission to defend themselves, and he put the Persian army and civil authorities at their disposal. Tens of thousands still tried to collect from the Jews and died trying. So did Haman's ten sons, whose bodies were hung on display.

Thinking himself clever enough to kill all the Jews in Persia, Haman was instead stupid enough to kill himself, his sons, and seventy-five thousand Persians as dumb as he was.

Learning from Haman's Mistake
Contagious Stupidity

The only time I was ever spanked in school, I didn't deserve it.

Gym was over for my first-grade class, and it was time to go back to our room. We boys lined up in one row on the long flight of stairs and waited for the girls to finish lining up on the other side of the staircase. Suddenly, the boys' line started moving. The kid at the front thought it would be funny.

Our teacher, a mean lady I'm very tempted to name, didn't agree. She ordered the boys to stand against the classroom wall, rear ends pointed out. She swatted her way down the line.

Stupidity is contagious in multidimensional ways. One dumb decision can affect a whole row of people. It can also prompt another stupid decision—enter the teacher, who under today's rules would have been fired.

God warned the early Israelites that if a person is dumb enough to reject him, "I will punish your children, and even your grandchildren and great-grandchildren" (Exodus 20:5). It's not that God is holding the innocent people accountable. It's that the consequences spread like a virus.

Before we do something stupid, it's a good idea to spend a little time considering how far the stupidity might spread.

HAMAN

No Question Is a Dumb Question

1. Haman determined that the Jews were inferior humans, worthy of extermination. How do we categorize and rate people today? What affect does that have on our nation and on individuals? Is it fair, for example, that people living in wealthy cities are able to send their children to schools funded by lucrative property taxes, when children in poor cities have to make due with lower-quality schools supported by fewer tax dollars? How does that fit with Jesus's teaching, "Love your neighbor as you love yourself" (Matthew 19:19)?

2. Haman worked up a high-profile plan to promote himself when he thought the king wanted to honor him. Why do some people seem to need more acceptance than others? When is it acceptable to promote ourselves? How can we know if the self-promotion has gone overboard?

3. Why do you think Jesus pushes people toward humility, and what value is there in cultivating a humble spirit? Think about some of the people you've known whom you admire most. Do they tend to be proud and domineering or humble and focused more on the needs of others?

4. Why do we enjoy it when bad guys like Haman get the noose? Would the ending be just as satisfying if Haman changed into one of the good guys? What do you think it would have taken to change Haman's character that radically? Is Haman that much different than any of us who have sinned?

5. In "Contagious Stupidity," we're asked to consider the consequences of dumb decisions, to think about how far the stupidity might spread. Haman's decision killed himself, his sons, and thousands of others. How far have you seen one dumb decision spread?

Haman Recap

DUMB DECISIONS	ROTTEN RESULTS
The king asks Haman's advice on how to honor an unnamed person. Haman assumes he's that person, so he suggests leading the honoree through the city on horseback.	The honoree is a Jew whom Haman hates, and the king orders Haman to lead the horse—as a servant.
Haman decides to kill the Jew he hates—and the man's entire race.	The plot backfires. Haman gets hanged, and the Jew gets Haman's job.

5
HOPHNI
AND PHINEHAS

Crooked priest brothers
ate prime cuts of God's sacrificial meat
and slept with the women who worked for them.

Let's say there's just one church you can attend. But the pastor steals from the offering plate and sleeps with the church secretary.

Would you keep going there?

That's the problem the Israelites faced.

Jewish law required them to worship God at one central location, which was in the heart of Israel. But the two main priests, brothers Hophni and Phinehas, were crooked and oversexed. They took sacrificial meat intended for God, and they slept with women who helped at the worship center.

LEFTOVERS FOR GOD

During the Exodus out of Egypt, Jews worshiped at a portable sanctuary, a tent called the tabernacle. When Moses and his people made camp, worshipers could bring their animal sacrifices to the altar outside the tent, in the curtain-walled courtyard. Once in Israel, though, the Jews set up a more permanent worship center in Shiloh located in the heart of the nation. That was the only place they were allowed to offer sacrifices to God.

"When you inherit the lands of these nations," God told the Exodus Jews, referring to the land that became Israel, "you must completely destroy all the places where they serve their gods. . . . Look for the place the LORD your God will choose—a place among your tribes where he is to be worshiped. Go there, and bring to that place your burnt offerings and sacrifices" (Deuteronomy 12:2, 5–6).

Shiloh became that place, though the worship center would later move twenty miles south to Jerusalem. If Jews wanted to ask God for forgiveness, they had to go to Shiloh and offer sacrifices. Many Jews from distant cities did this mainly on Jewish holidays, such as Passover or Pentecost.

As payment for their spiritual services, priests got some of the meat—at least from certain sacrifices. They got nothing from burnt offerings, since the entire animal was burned to atone for sin. But they did get part of the fellowship offering, which was presented as thanks to God for blessings such as a good harvest or recovered health. Friends and family would often join in the celebration meal. The worshiper and his group were allowed to eat everything except:

- the fat, which was burned as a sacrifice to God, and
- the breast and right thigh, which were given to the priests "as a gift" (Leviticus 7:31–32).

Hophni and Phinehas didn't follow these rules.

Connoisseurs of good food, they developed strategies for getting other cuts of meat, including the fat which helps season the meat during cooking.

Potluck

When sacrifices were cooked in a huge pot, the priests jabbed a big fork into the stew and fished around. "Whatever the fork brought out of the pot belonged to the priest" (1 Samuel 2:14). Potluck buffet.

Special Order

Sometimes the two wanted their meat raw, before anything was cooked. The priest's servant would tell the worshipers, "Give the priest some meat to roast. He won't accept boiled meat from you, only raw meat" (1 Samuel 2:15). Roasting was reserved for the Passover offering, as a way to remember that the Israelites had to cook their food quickly before rushing out of Egypt. Eating non-Passover sacrifices that way was dead wrong. It took a holy ritual and demoted it to a mere meal.

Off the Menu

Some worshipers resisted, insisting that the priests not take the fat intended for God: "Let the fat be burned up first as usual, and then take anything you want" (1 Samuel 2:16). That was more than fair—and sacrilegious enough, since God's law dictated exactly what cuts of meat the priests should get. They weren't supposed to get the worshiper's meat, and certainly not God's meat.

But in sacrilege overload, Hophni and Phinehas ordered their servant to get mean. "No, give me the meat now," the servant would reply. "If you don't, I'll take it by force" (v. 16).

Imagine church ushers bopping you on the head with the offering plate and taking the big bills out of your wallet.

Sleeping with the Help

Eli was their father and Israel's high priest. But he was growing old and was probably well over seventy by this time. Hophni and Phinehas must have felt they could get by with anything, since they figured one of them would soon replace their father as the highest official in Israel—a nation without a king.

In stunning disregard for their position as spiritual leaders, they had "sexual relations with the women who served at the entrance to the Meeting Tent" (1 Samuel 2:22). Phinehas was married, for the Bible mentions his pregnant wife. And given the importance of families in this culture, Hophni was probably married as well.

Adultery demanded the death penalty in ancient Israel. So Eli tried to talk sense to his sons. "Why do you do these evil things that the people tell me about? No, my sons. The LORD's people are spreading a bad report about you. If you sin against someone, God can help you. But if you sin against the LORD himself, no one can help you!" (vv. 23–25).

Bible experts aren't sure what Eli meant by that last statement. Perhaps he meant that God can settle disputes between people, much like a higher court does. But there's no one to appeal to if we offend God.

Or maybe he was thinking of Aaron's two sons, both priests. Nadab and Abihu did not prepare an incense fire as God had instructed, so God sent down fire and burned them to death. Then Moses said to Aaron, "This is what the LORD was speaking about when he said, 'I must be respected as holy by those who come near me; before all the people I must be given honor'" (Leviticus 10:3).

Whatever Eli meant, he saw trouble coming.

So did a prophet who visited him. "Why don't you respect the sacrifices and gifts?" the prophet asked, delivering a message from God. "You honor your sons more than me. You grow fat on the best parts of the meat the Israelites bring to me. . . . This must stop! I will honor those who honor me, but I will dishonor those who ignore me. The time is coming when I will destroy the descendants of both you and your ancestors. No man will grow old in your family. . . ."

"I will give you a sign," the message continued. "Both your sons, Hophni and Phinehas, will die on the same day" (1 Samuel 2:29, 30–31, 34).

A young boy named Samuel, who was being raised at the worship center as a child devoted to God's service, received a similar message from God. "I told Eli I would punish his family always, because he knew his sons were evil. They acted without honor, but he did not stop them" (1 Samuel 3:13).

To Eli's credit, he insisted that Samuel tell him the bad news, withholding nothing, and he responded with trust in God's judgment: "He is the LORD. Let him do what he thinks is best" (v. 18).

Learning from
Hophni and Phinehas's Mistake
Ministers Are Human

"My wife says I'm not a good enough person to be a pastor."

A friend of mine told me that over lunch one spring day. He resigned that autumn.

In fairness to his wife, he can be a difficult personality, occasionally confrontational and stubborn.

On the other hand, week after week he delivered the most consistently engaging, doze-proof sermons I've ever come across in any local church. And he has a compassionate heart; he's especially gifted at comforting people in crisis.

No congregation deserves a religious leader as lowdown and godless as Hophni and Phinehas. But no church should expect Saint Reverend the Holy either.

Ministers are like the rest of us: normal until you get to know them. Then the character flaws start popping up like chickweed on bluegrass. But before we plow up the lawn and resod, perhaps we should take a stroll across our own lawn and consider how we treat our own weeds: with patience and targeted care.

That's not to say we should spray weedkiller on our ministers. They need to tend their own yards—and we need to let them.

GOD'S MAGIC BOX

Sometime later—when Eli was ninety-eight years old, blind, and fat—war broke out between Israel and the Philistines. Israel lost the first battle, fought at Aphek, a city on the outskirts of what is now Tel Aviv. That places the battlefront only about a day's march from Shiloh, some twenty miles away.

Terrified that they would become slaves to another nation, the Israelites decided to call up God as a reinforcement. Their most sacred relic was the ark of the covenant, a gold-covered chest that held the Ten Commandments. Elders remembered that during the Exodus and the conquest, in the days of Moses and Joshua, this chest often led the way to victory. Soldiers marched with it into battle. The chest became physical evidence of God's presence among them, since the lid of the chest was considered God's earthly throne.

Hophni and Phinehas were caretakers of this chest, which was kept in the worship center's most sacred room. At the desperate request of commanders from the battlefront, the priests proudly took the chest to the Israelite camp, producing cheers as they arrived.

Philistines camped nearby heard the cheering and were horrified. "A god has come into the Hebrew camp!" they said. "Who can save us from these powerful gods? They are the ones who struck the Egyptians with all kinds of disasters in the desert" (1 Samuel 4:7–8).

Everyone was wrong—Philistines, Israelite soldiers, Hophni and Phinehas. God had not come to fight for the Israelites. Only a box made by human hands had come, and it offered no more help than a burst of false confidence.

Philistines routed the Israelites, who ran to their homes in the hills. Among the casualties: Hophni and Phinehas killed, and the ark of the covenant captured as a war prize. Philistines later returned the Ark, though, because disease seemed to follow it.

Old Eli, consumed with worry about the battle and the fate of his sons and the ark, sat in a chair by the side of the road waiting for news. It arrived with a fleeing soldier, who had torn his clothes and covered his head in dirt as sign of deep grief.

After hearing that the battle, his sons, and the ark were all lost, "Eli fell backward off his chair. He fell beside the gate, broke his neck, and died, because he was old and fat" (v.18).

Phinehas's widow delivered a son on what appears to be that very same day, when the people of Shiloh must have been worried about Philistines advancing on their holy city. She named the baby Ichabod, Hebrew for "no glory." She said it was because "Israel's glory is gone" (v. 21).

But so were the troublemakers. A new day was coming, led by a godly priest and prophet: Samuel.

Learning from
Hophni and Phinehas's Mistake
Christian Magic

When I was a youngster, I remember sitting on a West Virginia pasture beside my little brother, who was bleeding. We were waiting for Dad to rush the car to us and load my brother up for a trip to the hospital. Farm machinery had cut one of my brother's legs to the bone, just above the ankle.

My grandfather, not a churchgoing person, stood with us quoting a Bible verse. I discovered later that he believed if he quoted the verse and recited my brother's full name, the bleeding would stop.

That sounds bizarre, I know. But I don't think it's any more bizarre than other attempts to manipulate God into doing something we want him to do. We try to pump up our faith because we convince ourselves that if we have enough faith we can do anything. Jesus, by the way, promised that to the apostles and other early believers who, in fact, healed the sick and raised the dead. That doesn't mean Jesus intended believers throughout history to do the same. The miracles got people's attention and helped jump-start the church. But the healed people all died later.

I don't believe God wants us to pump up our faith muscles in the hopes of using them like a strong arm to take whatever we want. Nor does he want us to cling to religious objects or rituals that have lost their meaning and that offer only a false sense of security.

Samuel, the priest who followed Hophni and Phinehas, put it this way: "What pleases the LORD more: burnt offerings and sacrifices or obedience to his voice? It is better to obey than to sacrifice" (1 Samuel 15:22).

But even obedience shouldn't be treated as a way to manipulate God. We can obey. And we can ask God for help. After that, we can say with Eli—who got at least one thing right: "He is the LORD. Let him do what he thinks is best" (1 Samuel 3:18).

NO QUESTION IS A DUMB QUESTION

1. How do you think priest Eli could let his sons get so out of hand? What steps could an old priest like Eli have taken to correct such blatant misbehavior of his adult sons? Should he have followed the approach of former cable TV mogul Ted Turner who, during budget cuts, fired his son Teddy with the now-famous words, "You're toast!"? Why wouldn't Eli have done this, especially since he also raised Samuel, who became Israel's next priest?

2. What do you think Eli meant when he warned his sons that no one could help them if they sinned against God? Could he have been thinking about Aaron's two sons, priests who didn't

follow God's directions for incense offerings and who were killed by "fire . . . from the LORD" (Leviticus 10:2)? When Eli got messages from God that his sons would die, he seemed to reply with stoic acceptance. How would you have responded?

3. Do you think God honored the sacrifices of the worshipers, even though the priests were anything but godly? How does that relate to Christians today who feel betrayed by ministers who commit such blatant sins that they are expelled from the ministry?

4. If you could talk to the minister in the feature "Ministers Are Human," what would you say to him? What would you say to his wife? What do you think about the statement: "Ministers are like the rest of us: normal until you get to know them"? Assuming ministers have flaws like the rest of us, at what point do you think people in the church have a right to step in and confront the minister about them?

5. The Israelites tried to get God to help them win a battle by taking onto the battlefield their most sacred object, the ark containing the Ten Commandments. Enemy Philistines won the battle and took the ark as a war trophy. What are some ways we try to twist God's arm into getting something we want? Do you think it shows a lack of faith for us to ask God for something, and then to allow him the right to deny our request? Or does that simply acknowledge that he's smarter than we are?

Hophni & Phinehas Recap

DUMB DECISIONS	ROTTEN RESULTS
Instead of sacrificing the best meat to God, they eat it. In addition, they have sex with women who help at the worship center.	God vows to kill them both on the same day.
They take into battle the golden chest that holds the Ten Commandments—as if it's a magic box that assures victory.	Philistines crush the Israelites, capture the chest, and kill the brothers. When their father gets the news, he falls out of his chair, breaking his neck. Their family's priesthood dynasty dies with them.

6

JONAH

*His prophecy of doom jarred a city to repent but
he got so mad when God forgave them
that he asked God to kill him.*

Jonah's an incredible prophet for two reasons, and neither has to
do with a big fish.

- He had only a one-sentence prophecy that didn't come true.
- He did what few other prophets in the Bible could: he got
  people to repent. By doing that, he saved an enormous city
  from destruction.

That made him a success. But he felt like a failure because his
prophecy of doom vaporized. Nothing happened. He didn't care if
the people repented. He wanted them dead.

That made him a dummy because it shows he didn't have a
clue what kind of God he served. And that wasn't the first time
Jonah proved himself clueless.

RUNAWAY PROPHET

In fairness to Jonah, God asked him to do something that no person in his right mind would want to do.

Imagine Jonah as an Israeli rabbi today. He's taking a marathon walk to a neighboring Muslim country, where most of the people believe that Israel belongs to the Palestinians—and that the only good Jew wears a headstone instead of a yarmulke skullcap. The rabbi's mission is to go to the leading Muslim city and tell the people there that God will destroy that city in forty days. It would have to occur to the rabbi that it wouldn't take Muslim fundamentalists nearly that long to kill him.

Jonah's mission was to travel to Nineveh, a massive city near what is now Mosul, Iraq, along the Turkish border. Nineveh wasn't just any huge city; it was the leading city of Assyria—the empire that dominated the Middle East, including Jonah's tiny nation of Israel. Jonah had just a one-sentence prophecy to deliver, but it was an attention-getter: "After forty days, Nineveh will be destroyed!" (Jonah 3:4).

Jonah lived near Nazareth, in the Galilean village of Gath Hepher. From there, he couldn't possibly get to Nineveh by boat. He needed to follow the coastal and riverside caravan routes about a thousand miles northeast; he went southwest.

It probably took him three days to reach the port city of Joppa, some sixty miles away in what is now the twin cities of Jaffa and Tel Aviv. There, he booked passage on a ship that could do nothing but sail away from Nineveh. Jonah headed for Tarshish, a city that may have been in Spain or somewhere in northern Africa. Scholars aren't sure where it was; they're just sure it was in the opposite direction from Nineveh because that's the only direction the Mediterranean Sea went.

Jonah thought he could run away from God. Perhaps he believed, like many of his day, that gods ruled certain lands. Maybe Jonah thought God lived only among the Jews. After all, it was God who said of the Exodus Jews, "they will know that I am the LORD their God who led them out of Egypt so that I could live with them" (Exodus 29:46).

If so, Jonah may have thought that the moment he pushed off from Israel's coastline, he was in for clear sailing.

Jonah's brain wasn't rowing on all oars. Otherwise, a question would have occurred to him: if God had gone to Egypt to deliver his people, and if he parted the sea to bring them home, why would anyone think that geographical boundaries limited him—as though God worked for the port authority and couldn't do anything but wave after the ship set sail? Jonah was a dumb prophet. But God wasn't going to leave him dumb.

As easily as Jesus would later calm storms, God stirred one up. Sailors on Jonah's ship tried to save themselves by dumping cargo overboard, so the ship would ride higher in the thrashing sea. It didn't work.

They cast lots. That's perhaps a bit like pitching a flat stone painted on one side, heads for yes and tails for no. Figuring that someone on board must have angered a god, they worked through the crew and passenger list until they came to Jonah and got a yes. He was the source of the problem. To Jonah's credit, he admitted he was running from God, and he told sailors to toss him overboard.

Instead, they tried to row back to shore. But their muscles were no match for the wind.

"They picked up Jonah and threw him into the sea, and the sea became calm. . . . The LORD caused a big fish to swallow Jonah, and Jonah was inside the fish three days and three nights" (Jonah 1:15, 17).

Learning from Jonah's Mistake
You Can Run, but You Can't Hide

We all know people who run from God. Some of those people may be among our family and friends. And at times, we are the folks wearing the running shoes.

Runners know what God wants them to do. But they

don't believe it's in their best interest to do it. So they try ignoring God or going somewhere they hope they can lose him—places they can't imagine God wanting to be, and with folks they can't imagine God wanting to hang out with.

Jonah's story is in the Bible for one main reason: to teach us a bit about the relentless love of God. He's always pursuing us. Not like a stalker seeking some weird personal pleasure. But like a parent hunting for a lost child, for no reason other than to help. God never gives up on us, no matter where we run or how long.

For many people, I suppose, that's troubling because they'd just like to sail away and be done with God. But God knows what they're sailing into. So he pulls up a wave, or maybe a big fish, and he rides alongside.

When the person is ready to talk, he's right there. Always.

POUTING PROPHET

Usually, getting swallowed by a huge fish is a bad thing. But for Jonah, it saved his life.

The Bible, by the way, never calls it a whale—just a big fish. Jonah may not have gotten a good look at any part of the fish but its tongue and tonsils. As for Jonah's staying in the fish's belly for three full days, many scholars wonder if that was a poetic way of saying he traveled all the way to the place of death. Perhaps Jews thought it was a three-day journey to Sheol, the deep-down place where they said the dead went. If so, the writer's point could be that God brought Jonah back all the way from certain death, just as God later did for Jesus, who was buried in the ground for three days.

However long Jonah was trapped inside the fish, it was long enough to pray for help. God answered by having the fish vomit Jonah onto a beach.

Having learned lesson one—that you can't escape from God—Jonah set out for Nineveh. From the nearest beach, it would have been about six hundred miles away, following the most direct international trade routes. That's about a five-week walk, traveling twenty miles a day and resting on the Sabbath. That gave Jonah plenty of time to worry about how the Assyrians would take the news.

Assyria was one of the most vicious and violent empires in ancient history. Fine art considered worthy of decorating palace walls showed battle scenes of dead Jews impaled on stakes as thick as fence posts. Engraved in stone, some of that gruesome art has survived.

Jonah delivered his prophecy.

Jews—the race of people who knew God best—had a long history of ignoring God's prophets, even killing some of them. That's what makes the Assyrian response so incredible, because they knew nothing about God. "When the king of Nineveh heard this news, he got up from his throne, took off his robe, and covered himself with rough cloth and sat in ashes to show how upset he was" (Jonah 3:6). The king imposed a total fast, ordering the entire city—animals included—not to eat or drink anything.

"When God saw what the people did, that they stopped doing evil, he changed his mind and did not do what he had warned. He did not punish them" (v. 10).

What's a prophet to do after he warns a city of one hundred twenty thousand people that they're about to die—and they don't?

Jonah pouted.

"I knew that you are a God who is kind and shows mercy," he complained. "Please kill me. It is better for me to die than to live" (Jonah 4:2–3).

He went outside the city and waited, perhaps to see if his pity party would convince God to shower Nineveh in thunderbolts.

Instead, God grew a plant that shaded Jonah. Then God sent a worm that killed the plant and left Jonah shadeless. As the scorching sun rose, God added a blast-furnace wind blown in from the Iranian desert.

"Do you think it is right for you to be angry about the plant?" God asked.

"It is right for me to be angry!" Jonah replied. "I am so angry I could die!"

In the clincher that abruptly ends the book, God replies, "You are so concerned for that plant even though you did nothing to make it grow. It appeared one day, and the next day it died. Then shouldn't I show concern for the great city Nineveh, which has more than one hundred twenty thousand people who do not know right from wrong, and many animals, too?" (vv. 9–11).

What happened next? As far as we can tell, since the story ends there, Jonah said nothing. If that's so, it's the smartest thing he did at any point in his story. Silence would have been the intelligent response to the lesson God had been trying to teach him: mercy is available to anyone who calls on God, not to just the Jews.

Though Nineveh was eventually destroyed—wiped out by Babylonian invaders about a century after Jonah—God saved the generation that repented, just as he saved Jonah from the belly of the fish. We can only hope Jonah was smart enough to see the connection: that mercy available to him was mercy available for everyone.

Learning from Jonah's Mistake
The Chosen People

Jews don't have an inside track. They're not God's favorites. Never have been. If you're thinking they're the chosen ones, and the rest of us are the afterthought, sit a moment beneath a shade plant in the Iraqi desert to consider God's lesson for Jonah. The rest of us were God's goal all along.

Jews were the chosen ones in the same way Jonah was the man who took God's message to Assyria. Jews were messengers: "I will make you a light for all nations to show people all over the world the way to be saved" (Isaiah 49:6). But God's kingdom, mercy, and salvation are for everyone.

The rest of us aren't second-class citizens in God's kingdom. Salvation is salvation, whether it's for a very Jewish Jonah saved from a fish's belly or a very distant nation of non-Jews who ask God for help.

For those of us who think we're hopeless, that because of our sins we deserve to plunge to the depths of the sea in the belly of a fish or to be wiped off the face of the earth, we can take a lesson from Jonah and the Assyrians. God saved them both. He chose them both, and he chooses us. The apostle Peter once explained it this way: God "does not want anyone to be lost, but he wants all people to change their hearts and lives" (2 Peter 3:9).

We're not hopeless. We're chosen.

NO QUESTION IS A DUMB QUESTION

1. Why did Jonah run? Do you think he really believed he could get out of God's reach? What does running from God look like today? How do we run from God? Jonah ran because he didn't want to do what God told him. What are some things God tells us to do today that get people running?

2. When was a time you or someone you know ran from God but was pursued by God? How did God pursue the person, and what happened?

3. Why do you think the Assyrians accepted Jonah's prophecy and repented, when Jews rarely paid attention to the prophets?

Is the old saying true, that familiarity breeds contempt? Were the prophets so commonplace among the Jews that their words carried no more influence than any other religious leader in a system where leaders often disagreed? What does it take for God to get our attention about spiritual problems in our lives and in our land?

4. The Bible says that when the Assyrians repented, God "changed his mind" and didn't punish them. Some people wonder how an all-knowing God could possibly change his mind. React to this reply: "It wasn't God who changed. The people did. And when people change, God's plan for them changes, too."

5. God sent Jonah to Assyria because God cared about the citizens of what became one of the most vicious empires in human history. Who are some of the most vicious people, groups, and nations today? What does Jonah's story say about them? And what does it suggest our responsibility is to those hated people?

Jonah Recap

DUMB DECISIONS	ROTTEN RESULTS
God tells Jonah to warn Assyrians that their leading city will soon fall. Jonah books passage on a ship headed the opposite way.	Intercepted by God, Jonah ends up inside the belly of a huge fish.
Warning delivered, the people repent, and God spares all 120,000. Jonah complains that God made him look like a fool.	Jonah ends up sitting in the desert sun, asking God to kill him.

7

JEPHTHAH

*A warrior's only child danced out to greet him
when he returned from war, and he killed her to keep his
stupid promise.*

On the brink of war, Israelite commander Jephthah, desperate to win, made a ridiculous deal with God: "If you will hand over the Ammonites to me, I will give you as a burnt offering the first thing that comes out of my house to meet me when I return from the victory" (Judges 11:30–31).

What was he thinking? What "first thing" generally comes out to greet the man of the house after he has been away for a long time—at a war, no less?

It's hard to imagine any husband or father making a promise like that unless:

- every last drop of his compassion had been swallowed up by selfishness,
- every last drop of his wine had been chugged in a prebattle hunt for courage, or
- every last ounce of his common sense had been sucked from his brain to make room for testosterone.

Dumb as the vow was, Jephthah got dumber. He kept the vow. It's not as though he didn't have other options. He had several.

And a thinking man would have figured out at least one of them.

Oddly, one New Testament writer added Jephthah to the Hebrew Hall of Faith, perhaps because in spite of Jephthah's ignorance he truly did show faith in God (Hebrews 11:32). Equally odd is that given the reaction of Jephthah's daughter to news of her coming execution, she might actually have been OK with it.

SON OF A PROSTITUTE

Jephthah was the black sheep of his family—the throwaway. And that's what his family did with him. They kicked him out because he was only a half-brother—his father's son from a fling with a prostitute.

How they knew Jephthah was his father's son, when a prostitute generally has sex with lots of men, is unknown. Yet the Bible doesn't say they drove Jephthah off because they thought he might have been swimming in the wrong gene pool. Their motive was greed. They didn't want to split the family inheritance with him. That would have been doubly important if he had been the oldest son, since first sons typically got a double share of the inheritance.

Jephthah's family lived in Gilead, a Jewish-owned territory in what is now Jordan, east of Jericho. When his brothers ran him off, he moved to a land called Tob, perhaps on the Jordan-Syrian border about a two-day, forty-mile walk from his home.

"There some worthless men began to follow him" (Judges 11:3). Robin Hood and his not-so-merry men. "Mercenaries" is how some Bible experts describe them. "Robbers," "adventurers," and "misfits," according to others. This much is clear: they could fight.

Gilead's neighbor to the east, Ammon, launched an offensive to take back land they said the Jews stole from them three hundred years earlier. That was when the Jews, on their way from the Egypt Exodus, fought their way into the Promised Land.

Jewish elders in Gilead tried to find someone to put together an army and lead it into battle. No luck. They couldn't even bait anyone with the promise of ruling Gilead. So they turned to their misfit who already had at least a small army. They didn't, however, give him the same offer. They told him they would make him a commander, using a Hebrew word that refers to a military leader, not a political one.

As dumb as Jephthah was, he wasn't dumb enough to accept that measly offer—not when he had a monopoly on what they wanted most. "If you take me back to Gilead to fight the Ammonites and the LORD helps me win, I will be your ruler" (v. 9).

The elders agreed, launching Jephthah into Jewish legend as one of Israel's famous "judges," an elite group of leaders like Gideon and Samson who fought Israel's enemies.

With kingly style, Jephthah immediately sent an ambassador to Ammon to find out why they were attacking. When the king of Ammon said it was to take back land the Jews stole, Jephthah—again with kingly style— tried to negotiate. He offered the king a history lesson.

First of all, Jephthah correctly explained, the land of Gilead never belonged to the Ammonites. Instead, this region between the Arnon and Jabbok rivers had belonged to the Amorites. When Moses and the Hebrews arrived on the Amorite border, they asked for permission to pass through peacefully on their way to Israel. The Amorites responded with an attacking army. The Hebrews won. Jephthah explained that God gave this land to the Jews, who had paid for it in blood from a war they didn't start.

Once truth is on the table and obvious, there's not much left to say. The king of Ammon didn't respond. He ignored the history lesson and continued his war business.

Jephthah traveled throughout Jewish territories east of the Jordan River, apparently recruiting fighters. In time, he raised an army. He also received God's Spirit, given in rare cases in Old Testament times: "the Spirit of the LORD entered Jephthah" (v. 29).

Yet the army and the Spirit didn't seem enough for him. He still felt nervous. So he made a deal with God. If Jephthah's men won the fight, he would sacrifice the first thing out the door of his house to meet him on his return.

It was common in ancient times for animals to roam freely in and out of the dirt-floor homes. At night, many villagers protected their few animals by locking them inside the house with the family. So it's possible that Jephthah was hoping an animal would come out. But that's stretching it, considering how the Bible phrases the vow. Would a goat or a lamb come out to "meet" him?

Learning from Jephthah's Mistake
When Money Is Thicker Than Blood

It shouldn't come as a surprise that Jephthah's brothers drove him from home because of their greed—they wanted a bigger slice of the inheritance pie. We do the same thing today.

I'm the oldest of five kids. A few years back, I sat with Mom and her estate lawyer to witness Mom organizing her estate. She wanted to make it as easy as possible for her kids when it came time for us to settle her affairs. The lawyer offered one warning: make everything as clear as possible. If there's anything in particular that Mom wants to give to certain individuals, she should write it out on a list and include it with the estate documents.

Why so much detail? "Even the most loving families can get mean when it comes time to divide the property," he said.

Mom said if she thought her kids would act like that, she'd have us sell everything and give the money to charity.

> For Mom and Dad, leaving property for their kids was the least of their concerns. With Dad a retired factory worker and Mom a retired school teacher, they didn't have much for an accountant to tally. But what they desperately wanted to leave their kids was a legacy of love. They wanted us to love each other.
>
> Our parents wanted nothing to get in the way of that, least of all money. And I think most parents would agree.

VIRGIN SACRIFICE

"His daughter was the first one to come out to meet him, playing a tambourine and dancing" (Judges 11:34).

Jephthah's reaction tracks well with what we'd expect from a selfish person unwilling to take blame. Instead of admitting that he opened his big mouth one time too many and said something stupid, he blamed his daughter for being the first one out the door. "My daughter! You have made me so sad" (v. 35).

He's sad? She's the one who gets a knife blade taken to her jugular vein and then gets cut into manageable pieces and burned to ashes on an altar.

"Father, you made a promise to the LORD. So do to me just what you promised, because the LORD helped you defeat your enemies, the Ammonites" (v. 36). That's what his daughter said—evidence that stupidity is genetic.

Killing the girl was not Jephthah's only option. Here are several, from smartest to dumbest.

Option 1. Ignore it. Treat it as the nonbinding, illegal vow that it is.

God's law prohibits human sacrifice. Criticizing human sacrifice among pagan nations, Moses said, "The LORD hates the evil ways they worship their gods. They even burn their sons and daughters as sacrifices to their gods!" (Deuteronomy 12:31).

Option 2. Pay the $20 substitute fee.

"If someone makes a special promise to give a person as a servant to the LORD," that promise maker can be released from the vow by paying a fee to the priest (Leviticus 27:2). This law refers to people who are given as servants. But if this law is provided as a merciful loophole in comparatively minor situations, it should apply even more so for a deadly matter such as a human sacrifice.

"The price for a man five to twenty years old is about eight ounces of silver; for a woman it is about four ounces of silver" (v. 5). In today's market, when silver sells at $5 an ounce, four ounces would cost $20.

Option 3. Skip it and take whatever punishment you think may be coming.

Even if Jephthah thought his vow was binding and irrevocable and that God would punish him if he didn't do as he promised, he could have accepted the punishment. He could have paid the price for his own stupidity, instead of making his daughter pay.

Option 4. Sacrifice her, and earn a spot in history as one of the big dummies of the Bible.

Some scholars do, in fact, argue that Jephthah spared his daughter, perhaps requiring nothing more from her than virginity for the rest of her life. In what seems like wishful thinking, they read this between the lines. As the argument goes, the Bible says the young lady got her father's approval to "be alone for two months to go to the mountains. Since I will never marry, let me and my friends go and cry together" (Judges 11:37). When she came back, the Bible reports that "she never had a husband." But it also says, "Jephthah did to her what he had promised" (v. 39).

He had not promised her long life in a convent. He promised her as a burnt offering. The how-to of a burnt offering appears in Leviticus 1. A few graphic excerpts:

- Sacrificial animals were killed quickly by cutting the throat.
- "Skin the animal and cut it into pieces."
- "Lay the head, the fat, and other pieces on the wood that is on the fire of the altar."
- "Inner organs and legs must be washed with water."
- "Burn all the animal's parts on the altar."

It's impossible to imagine any father doing such a thing to his own daughter—and his daughter submitting. But these people lived in a culture where this kind of thing happened in the name of religion. And because the Old Testament at this time in history was probably passed along only by word of mouth, Jephthah may not have been as informed as we are about the other options available to him.

From our reading of the Old Testament, though, Jephthah's vow plunges well below stupid—and all the way to the bedrock bottom of tragic.

Learning from Jephthah's Mistake
Bloodshed in God's Name

We still offer human sacrifices as grisly burnt offerings.

Body parts have landed in the streets outside Jerusalem cafés and Iraqi storefronts—the work of fundamentalist Muslims invoking the name of Allah.

Mass graves of burned bodies scar Bosnia and Herzegovina—horrifying reminders of ethnic cleansing conducted by Christians as well as Muslims.

Holocaust memorials dot the globe in tribute to six million Jews buried, burned, or left to rot as a fragrant offering to the Bible's predicted thousand years of peace—renamed the Third Reich. At the time, much of the German church approved.

We lie to ourselves when we say our day is brighter than Jephthah's—unless it's brighter because more bodies are burning.

What's the role of a Christian in such a world? "My kingdom does not belong to this world," Jesus said shortly before he was executed in God's name. "If it belonged to this world, my servants would fight so that I would not be given over to the Jews. But my kingdom is from another place" (John 18:36).

For a time, however, we live in this place. While we are here, we're not fighters. We're lovers. Sometimes that may mean fighting to protect those we love—but love is always the motive. Love doesn't hurt people; it heals. Love doesn't start fires; it puts them out.

NO QUESTION IS A DUMB QUESTION

1. Jephthah's family booted him out, perhaps partly because he was an embarrassing reminder of their father's fling with a prostitute, but mostly to cut him out of the inheritance. Have you seen any families do the same kind of thing today, and if so, for what reasons? How do we typically shuffle unwanted people—family or not—to the side?

2. Jephthah tried to reason with the attacking king, but reason didn't work even when Jephthah backed it up with solid facts. Why do you think the king plowed on, even knowing he was wrong? Have you seen the same kind of thing happen with disagreements in families, in churches, or on the job? Is there anything else a person can do to break through that kind of stubbornness?

3. The Bible says God's Spirit entered Jephthah. That happened in only rare instances in Old Testament times, to

empower select leaders for special service. Why do you think God's Spirit would enter the likes of a mercenary? Do you think it depreciates the holiness of God when God links up with an outcast like Jephthah?

4. Jephthah didn't have to sacrifice his daughter. Why do you think he didn't select any of the other options available to him? When we make ridiculous promises to God in moments of desperation, do you think it's a sin to break them?

5. Jephthah sacrificed his daughter in God's name. People in recent history have slaughtered others in God's name—most recently in the clashes between Muslims, Jews, and Christians. Should we kill the killers in God's name? What do you think is a Christian response to fundamentalists of any faith who shed blood in an effort to impose their faith on other people?

Jephthah Recap

DUMB DECISIONS	ROTTEN RESULTS
Headed into battle, Jephthah vows that if he wins, he'll sacrifice the first thing that comes out of his house to greet him when he gets home.	His daughter—an only child—comes dancing out to greet him.
He decides to fulfill his vow.	He kills his daughter and burns her body on an altar.

8

JEZEBEL

Committing murder for a royal vegetable garden,
Israel's queen of mean got fed to the dogs.

Israel's queen of mean may have had excellent reason from the crib for growing into the most despicable, villainous woman in Bible history. A single word may have twisted this sister, contorting and distorting her character from day one. That word: *Jezebel.* Her name.

Born the daughter of a king near what is now Beirut, Lebanon, she got saddled with a name that in her native language seems to mean: "Where's the Prince?" As in the first words out of the mouth of her father watching her birth. As in, "I don't want a daughter."

It gets worse.

Princess Jezebel married crown prince Ahab of neighboring Israel, to strengthen ties between the two countries. Hebrews tweaked the pronunciation of her name just a tad, from *izebul* to *izebel*. And suddenly she had a new name: "Where's the Crap?" As in excrement. As in we don't even want to guess what her nickname was.

Whether or not her name had anything to do with it, she grew into an insanely vicious woman. When anger of that intensity marries the absolute power of a monarchy, the landscape gets redecorated with a new color: blood red.

A KILLER APPETITE FOR VEGETABLES

City officials today have a procedure for taking land from a citizen who doesn't want to sell it. They condemn the property, evict the owner, pay a price they insist is fair, and then confiscate the land.

Jezebel had a better idea. Instead of condemning the property, she condemned the owner. His name was Naboth, and he was unfortunate enough to have inherited some land just outside of Jezreel, a hilltop city overlooking the scenic Jezreel valley. King Ahab and Jezebel had a getaway palace there. Naboth grew grapes on his property. But Ahab asked to buy the land so he could plant a vegetable garden.

Naboth explained that he couldn't sell the property. It had been in his family for a long time. Ahab slipped into a silent depression. He even stopped eating.

Jezebel was stunned. Apparently where she came from, royalty got whatever royalty wanted. "Is this how you rule as king over Israel?" she chided. "Get up, eat something, and cheer up. I will get Naboth's vineyard for you" (1 Kings 21:7).

And she did, by working the system. She ordered the city leaders to find two men who would testify that Naboth criticized God and the king. Jewish law required two witnesses for a conviction. After the orchestrated trial, Naboth was stoned to death. Ahab confiscated the land at zero cost and apparently grew his vegetables.

This is one time he should have skipped the vegetables, because they came with a warning: "In the same place the dogs licked up Naboth's blood, they will also lick up your blood. . . . Dogs will eat the body of Jezebel in the city of Jezreel" (vv. 19, 23).

Ahab and Jezebel would both pay for the land with their blood.

Learning from Jezebel's Mistake
Going Too Far

Killing someone for vegetables is going too far, even for a vegetarian. Jezebel had no right to turn a human being into a bag of bones for a bag of beans.

Fortunately, most of us don't know a Jezebel—a cold-blooded killer with an appetite for fiber. Unfortunately, we all know people who have gone too far—people as guilty as Jezebel with a head of lettuce in one hand and Naboth's head in the other.

Some misuse their authority. Some misuse their knowledge. Some even misuse their gifts from God. Take a church vocalist I once learned about from several friends. Great voice, but a nasty leader of other great voices. Queen of the church's praise team, she tolerated no rival. She cut several of the best vocalists out of the volunteer ministry, silencing the gifts that God himself had given them. And when the music required a solo part or an echo, the queen vocalist usually took it as an occasion to raise rafters with her powerful voice. When the pastor occasionally overruled her by inviting others to sing during the offering or during communion, she fussed and criticized those singers.

As far as I know, she didn't kill anyone. But she did drive people out of that local church. And she damaged the emotions of some who stayed to wait her out. When it came time for peer reviews, she got toasted and tossed. Church leaders had known she was a difficult personality and were trying to mellow her out and teach her some leadership skills. But it wasn't until they read the reviews that they realized how difficult she had become.

The lady was still in the church, last I heard, and was still involved in the music ministry, but not as a leader. Perhaps in time her leadership skills will catch up to her musical gift. If they do, the music in that church could soar.

It's normal to want to use the gifts God has given us—

whether those gifts are musical talents, leadership savvy, or a bucketload of smarts. But when we use those gifts to lift ourselves up and to drop others in a hole, we've gone too far. We're Christians. We're not in the business of helping ourselves to whatever we want. We're in the business of helping others to whatever they need. The apostle Peter put it this way: "Each of you has received a gift to use to serve others. Be good servants of God's various gifts of grace" (1 Peter 4:10).

HOW TO START A NEW RELIGION

Jezebel was not a Jew—not by race, and certainly not by religion. She worshiped Baal, a god of fertility in family, field, and flock. He sent the rain for crops, and he made women and female animals fertile. Jezebel also worshiped Baal's mother, Asherah.

Many scholars say Jezebel was likely more than just a worshiper. The people in her native country probably followed a practice common throughout the ancient Middle East, appointing the king's daughter as high priestess. This assured that the royal family controlled the nation's politics and religion, both of which were potential sources of trouble for a ruler.

If Jezebel was the high priestess, she considered herself not only queen of Israel, but also the highest authority in her religion. Whether or not she followed this ancient custom, she certainly set out to crush the Jewish faith and to elevate Baal worship.

Step one for getting this done was to drive the Jewish religion into the ground and six feet under, so she started killing Jewish leaders. She did this during a three-year drought, perhaps blaming them for the drought and arguing that Baal was angry about the Jewish religion in his land, that he was punishing the people by withholding rain. Many died, but one hundred Jewish prophets survived the slaughter by hiding in caves.

Step two was to elevate the status of her prophets. Using money from the royal treasury, she funded and even fed a religious congress of four hundred fifty Baal prophets and four hundred Asherah prophets.

A Jewish prophet named Elijah took a bold stand against her. He challenged her eight hundred fifty prophets to a battle of the gods. Whichever god sent down fire from the sky to ignite a sacrifice, that's the god the Jews would worship. So it was God and his solitary prophet versus Baal and eight hundred fifty prophets. Not only did Jezebel's team have the numerical advantage, but lightning bolts were a specialty of the rain god Baal.

Jezebel's prophets prayed all day. As evening approached, Elijah called down fire with just a short prayer, "Prove that you are the God of Israel and that I am your servant" (1 Kings 18:36). Fire fell. God won.

At Elijah's command, the crowd of witnesses executed Jezebel's prophets, annihilating her religious congress—a fate she had planned for the Jewish leaders. Her holocaust had backfired.

Oddly, it takes a Jewish word to best describe the reaction of this Judaism-hating queen: *chutzpah*. It means "supreme self-confidence." Awestruck at God's power Jezebel was not. Instead, she was livid about Elijah's attack on her power. "May the gods punish me terribly if by this time tomorrow I don't kill you just as you killed those prophets" (1 Kings 19:2).

By that time the next day, Elijah was kicking up dust balls as he ran for the desert. He ran all the way to Mount Sinai, as far as three hundred miles south. There, God gave him a new and encouraging assignment: "Pour oil on Jehu son of Nimshi to make him king over Israel" (v. 16). The days of Ahab and Jezebel were numbered.

PRETTY DEAD

Ahab died from a battle wound, and his son, Joram, became king. That made Jezebel the queen mother.

It seems Elijah's successor, Elisha, is the one who actually anointed Jehu as the coup leader who would end Ahab's family dynasty. Or perhaps they both did, with Elisha telling Jehu that the time to strike had finally come.

Jehu commanded a military unit for Israel, protecting a trade route in what is now Jordan. But with the support of his chariot corps and cavalry, he abandoned his post and charged some forty miles west to Jezreel. A lookout saw them coming and sent word to the king, who promptly dispatched a rider to intercept them and find out if everything was OK. But at Jehu's invitation, the rider joined forces with him. A second rider did the same.

By this time, the lookout recognized Jehu by his driving profile: "The man in the chariot is driving like Jehu son of Nimshi. He drives as if he were crazy!" (2 Kings 9:20).

King Joram climbed into his chariot and rode out to meet Jehu, perhaps fearing that his commander carried urgent news about an approaching invasion force.

"Is all in order, Jehu?" the king asked.

"There will never be any order as long as your mother Jezebel worships idols and uses witchcraft," Jehu replied. Then he pulled out his bow and arrow and shot the king dead. Probably within moments, the lookout had gotten word to Jezebel.

It's hard to explain the queen mother's last act. Perhaps she expected to survive the coup. Or maybe she was a DNA-deprived steel maiden who never got the genetic codes for fear. In fact, many scholars say she was probably intending to take her last breath in regal style, without a trace of panic. Instead of reaching for a sword, she chose two other weapons: eyeliner and a hairbrush. Prettied up, she waited inside the palace beside a window.

When Jehu arrived with his cavalry behind him, Jezebel had just one sentence for him, but it was a zinger. "Have you come in peace, you Zimri, you who killed your master?" (v. 31).

Calling Jehu a *Zimri* was not very polite. It's like calling someone a Benedict Arnold or a Judas.

Zimri, like Jehu, once commanded a chariot corps for Israel. He led a coup, murdered the king of Israel along with every male heir to the throne, and then declared himself king. His reign lasted one week. Ahab's father, another commander, defeated this traitor and became king. So Ahab's family dynasty was started because of this loser's failure, and Jezebel was rubbing it in.

Jehu decided to rub her out.

Perched by the window, Jezebel was one bird that couldn't fly.

"Throw her down," Jehu called up to the palace servants (v. 33).

When she hit the pavement, her blood splattered on the palace wall and the nearby horses. Jehu led his cavalry over her body, and then he went inside the palace for a bite to eat. He later sent someone out to collect and bury her corpse, but the dogs had been eating too. All that was left of Jezebel were her skull, feet, and the palms of her hands.

When Jehu heard this, he reminded his colleagues of the earlier prophecy: "The dogs will eat Jezebel at Jezreel. Her body will be like manure on the field. . . . No one will be able to say that this is Jezebel" (vv. 36–37). Instead, they would be left hanging with the question that became her Hebrew name: "Where's the manure?"

Jezebel did, however, leave behind a monument by which the people could remember her. It was a temple dedicated to Baal. King Jehu turned it into a public toilet. It must have seemed fitting.

Learning from Jezebel's Mistake
Something to Remember Me By

Given the way Jezebel died, it looks as though she wanted to be remembered as regal, strong, and brave.

My dad didn't die anything like that.

I was there in those final moments. He lay in a coma on a bed that had been set up in his living room—the same living room where he used to take on all five of his young kids at the same time in wrestling matches.

Twenty-seven years of non-Hodgkin's lymphoma had finally whittled him down to a wisp of a man, frail and gaunt like a corpse discarded in a concentration camp. It was tough to see him that way, because even in his early seventies, he was still climbing trees with a chainsaw to prune branches and was still riding his Harley Hog.

A gifted handyman, he was always helping out his kids. I've seen my sister's husband cry only once. It was when he told me about something Dad did for him. My brother-in-law doesn't think himself particularly handy with fixing cars, and he had been worrying all day at work about how he was going to fix his broken-down car when he got home that night. "By the time I got home," he told me, "Dad had already been there and fixed it."

Dad did that kind of thing for all of us. I lived eight hundred miles from the rest of my family, and up until the final few years of Dad's life, he and Mom would drive out every spring. He wanted to do chores for me: power-spraying the deck, replacing brakes on the car, mowing my lawn, and of course pruning our trees with his chainsaw.

Dad may not have died looking regal, strong, and brave. But he lived that way. He never gave up fighting for life. If there was a treatment he could take, he took it—and he took so many chemotherapy, radiation, and experimental treatments that I lost count.

What a legacy of courage he left us. But more important is his legacy of love.

Love was why he fought so hard to live, even though the doctors had given him only six months. He wanted to be there for Mom, his kids, and his grandkids. He worried about what would happen to Mom after he was gone and who would help out the kids when they needed it.

I knew that worried him. We all did. And in the moments before he died, I tried to assure him. "Dad, we'll take of Mom. And we'll take care of each other too. We're going to love each other the way you loved us. So don't worry. We'll be OK."

Dad died a little after midnight, late in September.

Though our family is missing one important person, remarkably we're stronger for that very reason. We're living out Dad's legacy as a family more connected to each other, more aware of each other's needs, and more available to step in and help.

It's a legacy I want to leave to my kids. I think most of us do. But to leave it in our death, we have to build it into our life.

No Question Is a Dumb Question

1. What makes people grow into mean and vicious adults? What do you think could have contributed to Jezebel's mean streak?

2. How have you seen a person in authority abuse that authority? What would you guess led the abuser to think it was OK to do this? How did the victim react? If you can remember a time when you were the victim, how did you react?

3. Jezebel never seemed to mellow out. Neither did the music leader in the "Going Too Far" feature, even though church leaders tried to mentor her. What do you think it takes to

change a self-serving, meanspirited human being into a self-less and kind soul? How does God accomplish that, and what role do we play in the process?

4. How could Jezebel ignore God's power after such a dramatic miracle as the one that ended in the execution of her eight hundred fifty prophets? How does God reveal his power today—in ways that we ignore? Why do you think people can be so resistant to God?

5. What kind of legacy do you think Jezebel wanted to leave? What is her legacy? How do we remember her? Who is someone who's no longer alive whom you knew personally and admired? What about this person lives on in your memory—and perhaps in your attitudes and behavior? How do you want to be remembered? What do you need to do to leave behind that legacy?

Jezebel Recap

DUMB DECISIONS	ROTTEN RESULTS
She arranges the murder of a man so her husband, King Ahab, can confiscate his property and plant a vegetable garden.	God promises that dogs will eat her.
She kills hundreds of God's prophets in an attempt to wipe out the Jewish religion and replace it with her own.	God uses a miracle to show that he's the true god. Jews kill 850 of Jezebel's prophets.
She vows to kill Elijah, God's prophet who ordered the execution of her prophets.	God has Elijah secretly anoint a new king who will launch a coup, ending the dynasty of Ahab and Jezebel.
Minutes after her son is murdered in a coup, Jezebel pretties herself up, perches by a high window, and taunts the coup leader when he arrives.	At the coup leader's command, Jezebel's servants push her out the window. She dies, and dogs eat her corpse.

9

JUDAS ISCARIOT

*The betrayer could have asked for christ's forgiveness
and been saved instead of killing himself.*

Could it be that we got Judas all wrong? What if it wasn't he who, in one of the dumbest acts in human history, betrayed Jesus? What if it was Jesus who betrayed Judas?

Judas, along with most Jews of the time, may have seen it exactly that way. Based on what prophets had said about the coming messiah, most Jews expected a military leader who would drive out the Roman occupiers and become an honest-to-goodness king of the Jews— just like David, only new and improved.

Jesus came as a big surprise. No one expected a pacifist messiah who would teach Jews to obey the Romans and to turn the other cheek when somebody hit them.

And no one expected a messiah who would say, "My kingdom does not belong to this world" (John 18:36). That would have made the prophets look like deceptive advertising copywriters who declared in huge print, "GREAT KINGDOM COMING," and then added the disclaimer in small print, "You have to die to get there."

When we read Old Testament prophecies about the messiah, it's easy to see where Judas and the other Jews—including every one of the other disciples—got the idea that the messiah's kingdom would be on earth. They had no idea there could be anything better, until Jesus came along with the news.

Even then, no one seemed able to believe it until after Jesus rose from the dead to prove it. Tragically, Judas didn't live long enough to see that. He died ignorant.

The legacy he left is one of ignorance, corruption, and betrayal. If he made any valuable contribution to Jesus's ministry as one of the disciples, the Bible never says, perhaps because the bad so drastically outweighed the good. The Bible reports only shameful scenes from his life. And in scattered lists of the dozen disciples, it consistently names him drop-dead last—the disciple at the dirt-smeared bottom of the totem pole.

PROFILE OF A DUMB DISCIPLE

There's a lot of guessing about what kind of man Judas was and where he came from. The favorite guess among Bible experts is that he was a disciple outsider, the only one who didn't come from Jesus's home region of Galilee in what is now northern Israel.

The solitary clue comes from Judas's second name, "Iscariot." Disciples probably tacked that onto his name to distinguish him from the other Judas in their group. That second name most likely referred to the similar-sounding village where he came from, most experts suggest. His father carried the same second name: Simon Iscariot.

In English, Judas's full name would have read something like this: Judas, Man (*is*, Hebrew) from Kerioth. The Bible does the same kind of thing to distinguish Mary Magdalene (hometown, Magdala) from other women named Mary. Judas's hometown may have been in southern Israel or perhaps in Jordan; scholars aren't sure which. But Kerioth doesn't seem to have been a village in Galilee.

A less popular theory based on Judas's second name is that he was one of the Dagger Men—hard-core Jewish Zealots called Sicarii, from the Latin word for "dagger." They opposed Roman rule, assassinating Roman leaders and soldiers. Or perhaps the name is one that Gospel writers added later, to describe him as a "fraud" (*saqar*, Hebrew). These are just a few of many theories.

Whether Judas was an outsider, an assassin, or a fraud, the bigger question is this: why did Jesus choose him?

"I chose all twelve of you," Jesus said, "but one of you is a devil" (John 6:70).

Perhaps it took a devil to do a devilish thing. The Bible doesn't say that's why Jesus chose him. But some experts offer that as an idea: Jesus purposely chose the man who would not choose him.

MONEY LOVER

Before Judas rejected Jesus, he rejected Jesus's ideas. Jesus preferred treasure in heaven to treasure on earth. He once told a rich man, "Go and sell your possessions and give the money to the poor. If you do this, you will have treasure in heaven. Then come and follow me" (Matthew 19:21). The rich man walked away. Judas would have done the same thing.

Had he been willing to wait for a treasure in heaven, he wouldn't have stolen from the disciples' treasury on earth. The disciples' expenses, for needs such as food and lodging, were covered by donations from followers. Judas served as the group treasurer: "He . . . kept the money box, and he often stole from it" (John 12:6).

How dumb could he be? Did he really think the miracle-working Jesus didn't know about this? Nathanael became a disciple because of Jesus's ability to see what was done in secret. "I saw you when you were under the fig tree, before Philip told you about me," Jesus told Nathanael (John 1:48).

Even the disciples eventually figured out that Judas was dipping into the moneybag. That's why we read about it in the New Testament. The disciples also knew that sticky fingers is why Judas objected to the woman anointing Jesus's feet with twelve ounces of expensive oil. "This perfume was worth three hundred coins," Judas said. "Why wasn't it sold and the money given to the poor?" (John 12:5).

The three hundred coins were denarii—worth about a year's salary for a laborer. Adjusting that cost to today's market, using the average annual salary of a construction worker, we would have to pay more than $35,000 for this scented oil. Judas could have helped a lot of poor people with that kind of money—after helping himself.

Spikenard oil was outrageously expensive because it was made from the spikenard plant that grows in the Himalayan Mountains of northern India, some three thousand miles east. That was roughly a half-year caravan trip, one way. Amber in color, this scented oil would have bathed the feet of Jesus in the warm aroma of earth and woods.

Jesus stopped short of revealing what really irritated Judas about the "waste," yet he quickly silenced him. "Leave her alone. She did it in preparation for my burial. You will always have the poor among you, but I will not be here with you much longer" (John 12:7–8 NLT).

In fact, Jesus would be crucified in six days. And he would die late in the day, shortly before the sunset beginning of Sabbath. And that was too late for anyone to wash and anoint his body with oil. Jewish law prohibited doing work on the Sabbath. By the time Jesus's followers would get around to doing this, on Sunday morning, he wouldn't be dead anymore.

Learning from Judas's Mistake
What's Wrong with Money?

Let's face it: we Christians aren't singing the same tune Jesus did about money. He wasn't keen on it; we love it. He warned us that money can keep us out of God's kingdom: "I tell you that it is easier for a camel to go through the eye of a needle than for a rich person to enter the kingdom of God" (Matthew 19:24).

We, on the other hand, sometimes promote money as a way to buy privilege in God's earthly kingdom. How many buildings on Christian college campuses are named after poor people? Most I know of are named after rich donors. Same with add-on wings of large churches. And ditto for churches on the mission field, sometimes named after rich Christians who sent money for the construction. "I love rich Christians," one denominational leader told me. "They give more so we can do more."

That doesn't sound like much of a warning about wealth. It sounds like the counterpoint to Jesus. It sounds like rich folks aren't going to get knocked off their camels at all. They're going to get a red-carpet bypass around the needle's eye.

In fairness to rich Christians, I believe that's exactly what will happen to many of them. I'm talking about the selflessly generous who live out the advice of Jesus: "Don't store treasures for yourselves here on earth where moths and rust will destroy them and thieves can break in and steal them. But store your treasures in heaven where they cannot be destroyed by moths or rust and where thieves cannot break in and steal them. Your heart will be where your treasure is" (Matthew 6:19–21).

Still, we shouldn't forget the warnings. Money can become a deadly trap. "The love of money causes all kinds of evil," Paul wrote (1 Timothy 6:10). It caused Judas to steal from his associates, and it may well have been the motive behind his betrayal of Jesus.

For Christians, money probably isn't going to lure most of us into betrayal, robbery, or murder. But money can steer our camel to the nearest spotlighted stage, where we can dismount and take a bow.

Before our bow, Jesus offers one more word of caution: Be careful! When you do good things, don't do them in front of people to be seen by them. If you do that, you will have no reward from your Father in heaven. When you give to the poor, don't be like the hypocrites. They blow trumpets in the synagogues and on the streets so that people will see them and honor them. I tell you the truth, those hypocrites already have their full reward. So when you give to the poor, don't let anyone know what you are doing. Your giving should be done in secret. Your Father can see what is done in secret, and he will reward you. (Matthew 6:1–4)

SELLING OUT JESUS

As far as some Bible students are concerned, it's no coincidence that Judas sold Jesus out for thirty silver coins.

The Bible doesn't say what kind of silver coins they were, so the value is uncertain. But since they came from temple officials, one good guess is the stater, the most common coin Jews used to pay their annual temple tax. Thirty staters equaled one hundred twenty denarii; that's almost half of what Judas would have gotten for selling Mary's imported oil.

Greed is why Judas betrayed Jesus, some experts theorize. But it's just a theory because the Bible never tells the motive, probably because even the other disciples didn't know it.

There could have been other forces at work.

Demon Possession

"Satan entered Judas Iscariot, one of Jesus' twelve apostles. Judas went to the leading priests and some of the soldiers who guarded the Temple and talked to them about a way to hand Jesus over to them" (Luke 22:3–4).

Much the same thing happened later, at the Last Supper. "As soon as Judas took the bread, Satan entered him. Jesus said to him, 'The thing that you will do—do it quickly.' No one at the table understood why Jesus said this to Judas. Since he was the one who kept the money box, some of the followers thought Jesus was telling him to buy what was needed for the feast or to give something to the poor. Judas took the bread Jesus gave him and immediately went out" (John 13:27–30).

Yet Judas was no puppet. And Satan wasn't the string-pulling puppeteer marching him to the temple. Jesus made it clear that Judas was responsible for his actions. "The Son of Man will die, just as the Scriptures say. But how terrible it will be for the person who hands the Son of Man over to be killed. It would be better for him if he had never been born" (Matthew 26:24).

Another Jewish writing from that century may help explain what was going on between Judas and Satan (also known as Beliar). "If the mind leans toward evil . . . it accepts the evil and is ruled by Beliar" (Testament of Asher 1:8). Jews at the time the New Testament was written typically believed that a person had the power to choose which impulse to follow: good or evil. Judas chose evil.

Forcing a Revolution

Many say freedom drove Judas, that he wanted to force Jesus to stand up in front of the top Jewish officials and boldly declare himself the messiah. The timing for a revolt would have been perfect. Tens of thousands of Jews had come to Jerusalem for the annual Passover festival. Rallying behind a charismatic leader, they could have easily surprised and overpowered Roman soldiers.

Many Jewish writings of the day, including some of the famous Dead Sea Scrolls, show that after about a century of Roman occupation, the Jews were expecting the messiah to arrive at any moment.

Whatever Judas's motive, he left the supper table and made his way to the temple. He knew that Jesus planned to pray in a nearby olive grove called Gethsemane. So after giving Jesus and the disciples time to get there, Judas led the temple police to that spot. A kiss on the cheek, a traditional greeting in the Middle East even today, would identify Jesus as the target for arrest.

"Greetings, Teacher!" Judas said, kissing him.

"Friend," Jesus replied, "do what you came to do" (Matthew 26:49–50).

Temple officers took Jesus into custody. It was Thursday night. By nine o'clock the next morning, Jesus would be nailed to a cross.

STUPIDITY REGRETTED

After an all-night trial, Jewish leaders sentenced Jesus to death. They needed only Governor Pilate's approval for the execution.

Whatever it was that Judas wanted—cash, freedom, or perhaps revenge on Jesus for humiliating him a few days earlier—he got more than he bargained for. Clearly, he was horrified at what the Jews decided to do to Jesus.

After they turned Jesus over to Pilate early in the morning, Judas took his blood money back to the Temple.

"I sinned," he said. "I handed over to you an innocent man."

"What is that to us?" they answered. "That's your problem, not ours" (Matthew 27:4). Judas threw the money at them and left.

Jesus died that day. So did Judas. "He went off and hanged himself" (v. 5). Judas was sorry. But instead of asking forgiveness, which Jesus surely would have granted, Judas made one last stupid decision. Perhaps he felt legally bound to hang himself. One of the Dead Sea Scrolls from that time describes the legal punishment for betrayal. It's written on what has become known as the Temple Scroll: "If someone betrays his people to a foreign nation or causes evil against them, you should hang him from a tree and let him die."

Yet one sentence that Judas missed could have saved him. Jesus spoke it from the cross. "Father, forgive them, because they don't know what they are doing" (Luke 23:34).

Did Judas die guilty or forgiven? God knows.

What we know is that he died ignorant. He didn't know that Jesus had spoken those words of forgiveness. He didn't know Jesus would be off the cross, out of the tomb, and walking again in less than forty-eight hours. And he didn't know that God would use the betrayal of Jesus as a catalyst that would spark a spiritual freedom movement that would change the world forever.

Learning from Judas's Mistake
Underestimating God's Forgiveness

You know one of the toughest things to believe in? Tougher than believing in an invisible God or an unimaginable heaven, or even something as incomprehensible as eternity?

Forgiveness.

Some of us can't believe God would ever forgive us because we can't forgive ourselves, and neither can the people we've hurt.

Unforgiven, we:

- drove away our child with our never-ending criticism;
- gambled away our savings;

- destroyed our family through adultery;
- sexually abused someone;
- aborted an unborn child;
- drank and drove and killed;
- shot civilians in a war.

Try as we do, we can't forget. Even in fleeting moments of relief, the most surprising associations can jar us back to the pain: we see a mother playing with her child, or we catch the scent of a rose, or we hear a familiar song on someone's radio.

With the pain inescapable by day, we long for the night and hope for respite in our sleep. But nightmares retreat with us.

How could God forgive us for a sin that plunges that deep?

Judas must have thought the same, for he killed the Son of God. He was as guilty as the Jewish officials who convicted Jesus and as guilty as Pilate who sentenced him and the executioner who nailed him to the wood.

And yet while Jesus took his dying breaths, he spoke the words that revealed God's sole reason for sending him: "Forgive them."

What sin could be greater than killing the Son of God? And if there is forgiveness for that, what sin could be unforgivable—aside from the sin of having no remorse?

Not only could God forgive the most terrible sin in human history, he allowed that sin for the very purpose of showing that forgiveness is more powerful than sin. Jesus said as much a few hours before he died: "This blood is poured out for many to forgive their sins" (Matthew 26:28). If we've sinned and we're sorry, there's forgiveness.

NO QUESTION IS A DUMB QUESTION

1. There are a lot of theories about why Judas betrayed Jesus. Which one makes most sense to you, and why? If Judas were trying to force Jesus into launching a rebellion, can you understand why Judas did that? Can you think of a situation when it's appropriate to apply pressure to get someone to do something they wouldn't otherwise do? What's the risk of doing that?

2. Think about betrayals you've seen or perhaps experienced. What caused them, and what were the results?

3. Jesus and the disciples needed money. But Judas's need warped into greed. How can we tell when need becomes greed? What are some common symptoms?

4. Jesus couldn't protect himself from a defector—from Judas, who was determined to reject him. What message does that send to churches and to Christian parents who blame themselves for bad choices made by their fellow members or their children? When we publicly compliment the parenting skills of someone whose child turned out well, how do you think that affects parents who have a troubled child?

5. Why do you think Judas killed himself instead of asking forgiveness? Do you think he was covered by Jesus's prayer from the cross, in which Jesus forgave the people who killed him? Of the people you've known and the sins you've seen committed, what were some of the ones that seemed hardest to forgive? How would you advise a friend who is consumed with guilt to accept God's forgiveness?

Judas Iscariot Recap

DUMB DECISIONS	ROTTEN RESULTS
He criticizes a woman for anointing Jesus with expensive oil, saying the oil should be sold and the money given to the poor.	His reputation is tarnished by the implication that he wants the money for himself. He's the group treasurer, and he steals from the group fund.
For a price, he shows Jewish authorities where they can arrest Jesus when crowds aren't around to violently protest.	Jesus is executed. Judas, apparently horrified by this, kills himself.

10

PHARAOH OF THE EXODUS

Even after ten horrifying plagues
prove that God wouldn't take no for an answer,
Egypt's king had a thick-headed relapse.

It's hard to know where the king of Egypt's dumbness started.

Did it start when he said, "Let us deal shrewdly with them" (Exodus 1:10 NKJV), and then he came up with a bunch of simple-minded ideas for controlling the exploding Hebrew population—ideas that made the earlier baby boom look like a baby beep?

Or did it start several decades later, when he told Moses to practice his magic tricks on someone else—"magic tricks" now famous as the ten plagues?

There's enough stupidity here for two kings. In fact, there probably were two kings. The Bible never bothers to tell us their names but simply calls them by their formal title: Pharaoh. Yet their stories are at least eighty years apart.

King number one got worried that the Hebrew immigrant population was out of control. So he came up with a plan.

Plan A. Enslave the Hebrews and tried to work off their energy so they wouldn't have as many kids. But the exercise invigorated them, and the birth rate soared.

Plan B. Hebrew women who delivered babies for their people were to kill the newborn boys. These women, however, feared God more than the king.

Plan C. All Egyptian patriots were to help with homeland security by throwing Hebrew baby boys into the Nile River.

Enter Moses, floating.

Smarter than Egypt's king, the mother of Moses managed to fulfill both her patriotic duty and her motherly duty. She put baby Moses into the Nile, but she protected him in a waterproof basket and placed him near where the king's daughter bathed.

The princess took him home.

One brick shy of a great idea, the king who intended to put the Hebrews in their place actually raised in his own home the man who would lead them to the Promised Land.

LET MY PEOPLE GO

Moses left Egypt when he was forty years old, and he returned at age eighty with a message from God: "Let my people go" (Exodus 5:1).

Bible experts get pretty worked up arguing about which Egyptian king Moses was addressing. That's because there aren't many clues in the Bible or from archaeological discoveries about who the king was, and what clues do exist can be interpreted different ways.

Some experts say Moses may have been confronting a warrior king nicknamed the Napoleon of Egypt: Thutmose II, in the mid-1400s BC.

Others say Moses delivered God's demand to an egomaniac who built more statues of himself than Donald Trump built towers: Rameses the Great, in the mid-1200s BC.

Whoever the king was, he had granite for brains.

"I will harden his heart," God warned Moses (Exodus 4:21 NKJV).

God meant his head. "I will make the king very stubborn, and he will not let the people go."

The question is how much help did God really need to give the king? Totalitarian monarchs of the Middle East were no butterflies, easily diverted to flights of someone else's fancy. They did what they wanted—Egyptian monarchs even more so. They rose with divinity in their wings, or so they thought. They were considered gods, sons of Ra, who was the powerful sun god in this desert land. That's why the king answered Moses the way he did. "Who is the LORD? Why should I obey him and let Israel go? I do not know the LORD, and I will not let Israel go" (Exodus 5:2).

The supposed god Pharaoh considered himself fully aware of other gods in the Egyptian gallery. But he didn't know who Moses was talking about. Pharaoh wasn't about to jeopardize Egypt's economy by releasing the nation's main source of cheap labor—all on the word of some unknown God.

To stamp an exclamation point on his outrage at such a request, Pharaoh ordered the Hebrews to start chopping their own straw. They needed the straw as a binding agent that held together the mud bricks they were forced to make for Egyptian building projects.

He'd show them who's god.

BATTLE OF THE GODS

When Moses went back to the palace, the king asked him to perform a miracle, probably to prove that Moses represented a real god. Aaron, older brother of Moses, threw down his walking stick and it turned into a snake.

No big deal, the king must have thought. It looked like a snake charmer's trick—one still used with the Egyptian cobra, *naja haje* species. These poisonous snakes often grow three to six feet long but can reach nine feet. Pressing on the nape of the snake's neck apparently pinches a nerve and can suddenly turn the snake stiff and motionless. To revive the snake, all you have to do is toss it on the ground.

Magicians in the palace did the same thing Aaron had done. The difference was that Aaron's snake ate theirs for breakfast. That was the king's first clue that he should start paying attention. But he remained clueless. What followed were ten plagues, one after another, devastating Egypt.

Though these plagues would gradually wear down the granite-headed king, that wasn't their main purpose. Fact is, God strung out the process by stretching the king's stubborn streak. After each plague, the king could have freed the Hebrews. But the king continued to refuse, with God's help.

God was putting on a show—a faith spectacle. Not for the king but for the Hebrews who had been living in Egypt four hundred thirty years. God had promised their ancestor, Abraham, that he would make the Hebrews into a great nation. The time had come for God to deliver on that promise. He began by introducing himself to his people.

Pharaoh had wanted to show everybody who was god. And through his stubbornness, that's exactly what he would do.

Many Bible experts speculate that in the choice of plagues, God targeted many of the Egyptian gods, including Pharaoh. Some experts also suggest that God used a series of natural disasters—beginning in autumn of one year and stretching through spring of the one following—with each disaster triggering the next. If so, the plagues fell one after another like a row of dominoes.

Here's a list of the ten plagues, along with some of the many gods that could have been targeted, and the possible natural causes.

1. Nile River turns red

Target god: Hapi, god of the autumn flood that irrigated the riverside fields.

Natural cause: Heavy flooding carried decayed, toxic algae (Red Tide) from the swamplands upriver. Excerpt from an Egyptian story in the 1300s BC: "The river is blood. People refuse to drink it, and thirst for water."

2. Frogs

Target god: Heqet, frog-headed goddess of childbirth.

Natural cause: Frogs fled the polluted river.

3. Insects

Target god: Shu, god of the air.

Natural cause: Perhaps mosquitoes or gnats bred in pools left by the receding flood.

4. Flies

Target god: Beelzebub, a regionwide fertility god known as "lord of the flies."

Natural cause: Possibly the stable fly, which lays eggs in wet, decaying substances such as dead frogs and wet grain.

5. Diseased livestock

Target god: Hathor, queen of heaven and goddess of fertility, portrayed as a cow.

Natural cause: Possibly anthrax, African horse sickness, or Bluetongue virus, each carried by insects.

6. Boils

Target god: Sekhmet, goddess who could send and cure disease.

Natural cause: Skin anthrax carried by insects, producing blisters and boils.

7. Hail

Target god: Tefnut, goddess of water and weather.

Natural cause: Hail is common in Egypt. The crops destroyed would have been growing in January and February.

8. Locusts

Target god: Termuthis, god of harvest.

Natural cause: Migrations can arrive from fall through spring, though they are usually controlled today by pesticides.

9. Darkness for three days

Target god: Ra, the sun god, king of gods, and father of the pharaoh.

Natural cause: The hot khamsin winds blow in from the Sahara Desert any time from March through May, forcing drivers today to use their headlights.

10. Death of oldest child

Target god: Pharaoh, whose own son died in this plague.

Natural cause: The oldest children got special treatment and may have eaten more contaminated food than the others. Oldest animals died, too, however.

The king nearly gave in several times. After his magicians couldn't get rid of the frogs, he told Moses, "Pray to the LORD to take the frogs away from me and my people. I will let your people go" (Exodus 8:8).

The frogs went, but the Hebrews didn't. Pharaoh wouldn't let them. The Bible says he got stubborn again.

Ditto after the plague of flies, then hail, then locusts. The king tried to negotiate a deal during the plague of darkness, to let the Hebrews go without their animals, but Moses said that was a deal-breaker.

It wasn't until the tenth plague that the king finally gave in. God sent an angel of death, who killed the oldest child in every Egyptian household, but who passed over the Hebrew houses. This tragic miracle that won freedom for the Hebrews is one the Jews remember each spring during their Passover holiday. God showed Pharaoh who was God.

"Get up and leave my people," the king told Moses that night. "You and your people may do as you have asked."

Egyptian citizens urged the Hebrews to hurry: "If you don't leave, we will all die!" (Exodus 12:31, 33).

The Egyptians were so happy to see the Hebrews go that they gave them parting gifts—anything the Hebrews wanted. And they wanted a lot. They asked their Egyptian neighbors "for things made of silver and gold and for clothing" (v. 35). They might have been slaves, but they were no dummies.

Pharaoh, on the other hand, was a slow learner. And he needed one more painful lesson.

ON SECOND THOUGHT

Moses led the Hebrews east, toward the Martian-like badlands of the Sinai Peninsula—the not-so-scenic route to what is now Israel. The shorter route followed the Mediterranean coast, on a caravan road called the Way of the Philistines. But stationed along the roadside were Egyptian outposts. Moses didn't want his fugitives fighting battles they could avoid.

The Bible doesn't say how far into the trip the Hebrews got before the king had second thoughts. But it must have been long enough for things to have settled down in Egypt.

"What have we done?" the king and his advisers said. "We have let the Israelites leave. We have lost our slaves!" (Exodus 14:5).

The king called for his war chariot, and then mustered his entire chariot corps. He led the chase, followed by his elite corps of six hundred chariots and all other chariots at his disposal. Egyptian art shows that each chariot was usually manned by three soldiers. The king had put together a substantial force, fully capable of functioning like sheepdogs with spear-tipped teeth, to herd the Hebrew refugees back to Egypt.

In fairness to the king, it wasn't entirely his decision to challenge the Hebrews and their God one last time. The Lord had told Moses, "I will make the king stubborn again so he will chase after them, but I will defeat the king and his army. This will bring honor to me, and the Egyptians will know that I am the LORD (v. 4). So would the Hebrews—as well as the rest of the world.

News of the miraculous way God defeated the Egyptians would spread throughout the Middle East, terrifying Israel's enemies for decades. And, for the Jews, memories of this miracle imbedded steel into their faith. This miracle proved that they were the chosen, backed by God himself.

Pharaoh caught up with the Hebrews while they were camped beside a sea. There was nowhere for the Hebrews to go but through the chariot corps or through the water.

Exactly which body of water blocked them remains a matter of debate. The Hebrew words for the sea are *yam sup. Yam* means sea, but what's *sup* mean? It can mean "reed," "far," or even "swept away." So it could have been the Faraway Sea, a way of describing the Red Sea far from Egypt's population centers along the Nile River. Or it could have been the Reed Sea, referring to one of the many freshwater lakes in the area where reeds grew along the banks. Or it could have been the Swept Away Sea—a pun describing whichever sea it was that God swept apart for the Hebrews and then collapsed onto the Egyptians, sweeping them away.

After the Hebrews left Egypt, a glowing pillar of light began to lead them. But now that the Egyptians had arrived, this light beam moved behind them as a rear guard, blocking the chariots. Meanwhile, a hot east wind started blowing in from the Arabian Desert, continuing all night long and eventually parting the water.

Scientists studying the northern tip of the Red Sea, in the Gulf of Suez, have calculated that it's possible for a steady wind blowing all night to push back the water, exposing a reef or a sandbar. Once the wind stops, the water would rush back within about half an hour. Such reports have appeared in the *Bulletin of the American Meteorological Society* and the *Bulletin of the Russian Academy of Sciences.* However God cut a path into the water, this miracle became the most memorable in Jewish history, and the Hebrews walked across the dry seabed.

The Egyptians followed. They could have done nothing dumber. They had lived through the plagues that targeted them but avoided the Hebrews. They had stood all night behind a light beam from heaven that blocked them from getting at the fugitives. And they had watched the Hebrews escape through a path blown into the sea.

And they thought it was safe to follow?

"Moses raised his hand over the sea, and at dawn the sea returned to its place. The Egyptians tried to run from it, but the LORD swept them away into the sea. The water returned, covering the chariots, chariot drivers, and all the king's army that had followed the Israelites into the sea. Not one of them survived" (Exodus 14:27–28).

The only Egyptians who escaped were those who might have been watching helplessly from the shoreline.

We don't know if the king was among the casualties. The Bible doesn't say. Neither do any of the Egyptian records discovered so far. If he did die, it was his stupid arrogance that killed him. If he didn't, perhaps he learned his lesson—for the Hebrews never had any more trouble from the Egyptians during the rest of their trip home to the Promised Land.

Learning from Pharaoh's Mistake
Stubborn to the Bone

Stubbornness isn't all bad. It comes in handy and healthy sometimes.

Take teenagers—a mass of humanity that seems more like a herd of mousy lemmings charging over the nearest cliff. Peer driven, teens can follow the crowd deep into danger. They can:

- drive like a toddler strapped to an Indy racecar;
- discover what it feels like to get drunk;
- smoke to look cool;
- have sex for bragging rights;
- take drugs to cultivate that bad-boy, bad-girl mystique.

Teenagers who can consistently say no to such invitations from their friends certainly earn the admiration of grownups who remember how much they craved acceptance in their younger days.

Stubbornness can come in handy for adults too. Like teenagers, we get asked to do dumb things. Often the dumbness has to do with lying to cover up someone else's dirty deed, a bit like sweeping dirt under a rug instead of admitting the spill and cleaning it up. The dirt is the deed, and the rug is the lie. And if we agree to the lie, it's our reputation that gets trampled.

On the other hand, stubbornness gone overboard can be just as damaging. One elderly lady I know of and her frail husband live together in a home they can no longer maintain. Her husband has had several strokes and heart attacks, and is paralyzed on one side of his body. Yet he drives his wife to church and the store because she never learned to drive. This couple's adult kids have tried for years to talk them into a retirement center. He's willing, but she's not. One more disabling stroke or heart attack, and the couple will have little choice.

The kids worry that their mother's stubbornness is placing both parents at risk. And they worry that when their parents have no choice but to move into a retirement center, the pickings will be as slim as their savings—drained by ongoing home improvements.

"Those who are stubborn will get into trouble," warns a sage from ancient Israel (Proverbs 28:14).

If we're not the stubborn person, sometimes there's little we can do but make our case and then watch and pray.

But if we are that stubborn person, we have the option of swallowing our pride—with a spoonful of common sense, a bucket of counsel from the people who care about us, a truckload of God's grace, and if necessary a tiny pill to level out the chemical imbalance that tips our brain to the south side of stubborn.

No Question is a Dumb Question

1. The Egyptians grew to fear the exploding population of Hebrew immigrants. Sound familiar? Why do some people in the native majority of any country tend to fear a minority group on the grow? What tends to keep racial groups segregated from each other? Is the segregation inevitable, or are there ways to bridge the barrier? What are the advantages and disadvantages of doing this?

2. We would be hard-pressed to find any human being more stubborn than Pharaoh of the Exodus. But let's try. Who is a stubborn person you've known or perhaps heard about? What examples show they are stubborn? What do you think makes a person so rigid and unwilling to change, even when the stakes are high? How have you seen people hurt by stubbornness that overwhelms common sense?

3. What's the best way to help a person like that? How would you advise the adult children of the elderly couple in "Stubborn to the Bone" to help their parents? How can you protect yourself from someone with a stubborn streak, especially if you live with a person like that?

4. In some cases, the Bible says, God made the king of Egypt stubborn and resistant to the miracles that Moses per-

formed. So the plagues may have lingered longer than they would have otherwise. People died because of that. Do you think God really made the king more stubborn, literally? Or was that a figurative way of saying God used the king's ingrained stubborn streak? If God really did make the king do things that ended up killing people, how can we justify God's doing that? For Christians who believe in free will—that God lets us choose our own eternal destiny, and that he wants us all to be saved—how would they justify this story? React to this response to that question: "God is determining how the Egyptians die, not their eternal destiny. It's their choice whether or not to reject God."

5. Would it bother you if most of the ten plagues were caused by natural disasters? Do you think the idea that they were is plausible? Some people say that attempting to explain miracles is a trick to deny the power of God. Do you agree? Some Bible experts say that looking for explanations about the "how" of miracles is missing the point—that the stories are told to reveal the "who," which is God. Do you agree?

Pharaoh of the Exodus Recap

DUMB DECISIONS	ROTTEN RESULTS
He refuses God's demand to free the Hebrews.	His nation is devastated by ten plagues, the last of which takes the life of his oldest son.
After freeing the Hebrews, he changes his mind and leads his chariot corps to bring them back.	They drown in a flood.

11

NABAL

Only a man named Fool
would insult an army of six hundred hungry men
camped in his own backyard.

Y ou've got to wonder about parents who look into the eyes of their newborn son and name him Fool. That's what "Nabal" means in the Hebrew language. Bible experts wonder about those parents too.

Some argue that there's no way parents would give a kid a name like that. The scholars speculate that "Nabal" was a name that some editor substituted later because it so perfectly describes the character of this big dummy. So these experts allow for a little poetic license in the story, and poetic justice for the villain.

Other experts say, "Not so fast." Perhaps his real name was a similar sounding word, like *Niblu*, an Akkadian name from what is now Iraq. It means "child" or "descendant." Maybe his wife just called him Nabal when it came time to criticize him because the two words sound so much alike—an obvious disparaging pun.

There's another possibility: his parents really did name him Fool.

There are plenty of people in the Bible with names that no chemically balanced human being would ever wish upon a child.

Naomi had a knack for coming up with them. She named her

sons Mahlon (Sickness) and Kilion (Destruction). And when this lady who sounds like she needed happy pills wound up widowed and sonless, she called herself Mara (Bitter). Then there are prophets who gave their children symbolic names, the longest of which is Maher-Shalal-Hash-Baz. It literally means Swift-Spoil-Quick-Plunder. It pointed to Isaiah's prophecy that two nations attacking the Jews would themselves soon be invaded and plundered. We can only hope Isaiah gave his boy a more compassionate nickname. Perhaps Swifty (Maher).

As for Nabal, whether or not that was the real name of this particular dummy, it was certainly his real character.

GIVING A BUZZ OFF AT SHEEP SHEARING

Nabal was a sheep and goat man—a rich one. He owned three thousand sheep and one thousand goats. As his story begins, he's enjoying his wealthiest season of the year: springtime sheep shearing. That's like harvest time for wheat farmers today, when they sell off the grain and roll in the dough.

The wool of three thousand sheep was no small change. It would have paid three years of taxes that the entire nation of Moab, in what is now Jordan, had to pay to Israel (2 Kings 3:4).

Sheep shearing became a working festival: lots to do, but with plenty of food and celebration. Relatives and friends often came to enjoy the festivities. It was a happy time because it was a wealthy time. Nabal wasn't hurting.

David and his growing army, however, were. Fugitives on the run from an insane King Saul, they were holed up in rocky badlands near the Dead Sea—the Desert of Maon. That's about twenty-five miles south of David's hometown, Bethlehem. Nabal lived on the northern edge of the badlands, in the village of Maon. And he was shearing his sheep just a mile farther north, in Carmel.

Hearing about the festival, David sent ten of his men up to kindly ask Nabal for some supplies. Apparently during the winter, Nabal had grazed his flocks in the warmer southland fields near where David's army was hiding. David's soldiers protected the shepherds and their flocks, asking for nothing in return—and getting what they asked for.

As one of Nabal's shepherds put it, "These men were very good to us. They did not harm us. They stole nothing from us during all the time we were out in the field with them. Night and day they protected us. They were like a wall around us while we were with them caring for the sheep" (1 Samuel 25:15–16). Nabal certainly would have known that. Any fool would have.

Yet Nabal not only rejected the request like most of us do with door-to-door solicitors; he insulted the men. "Who is David? Who is this son of Jesse? Many slaves are running away from their masters today! I have bread and water, and I have meat that I killed for my servants who cut the wool. But I won't give it to men I don't know" (vv. 10–11).

Nabal essentially called David a big nobody who wanted to be a somebody and thought he could get there with runaway slaves. In fact, runaway slaves and debtors were among David's soldiers: "Everyone who was in trouble, or who owed money, or who was unsatisfied gathered around David, and he became their leader" (1 Samuel 22:2).

Still, what Nabal did was worse than criminally inhospitable—returning evil for good in a culture that demanded hospitality to strangers. It was stupid. What person in his right mind would deliberately insult an army of six hundred men camped in his own backyard, no more than a few hours' march away?

A man named Fool.

Learning from Nabal's Mistake
How Much Is Enough?

Living in the Kansas City suburbs, I remember how easy it was to beat up on KC Royals' first baseman George Brett in the early 1990s when he was negotiating those two- and three-million-dollar salary deals. Especially after he answered a reporter's question about how much is enough. He said you never have enough. Apparently not.

Top baseball players today are drawing salaries about ten times as much—well above the twenty-million-dollar range. And top corporate officers are playing ball, too, with salaries out of the ballpark while their employees live off hot dogs.

There's incredible disparity between them and us. But a trip to some inner cities, some rural communities, or to any number of developing nations reveals the flip side of the coin. Average workaday grunts like us are the wealthy ones. We are "them."

As Christians, it's not our job to tell the richer-than-us how to mind their business. It's our job to mind our own business.

God, throughout the Bible, repeatedly asks us to help people who are thrashing about in a desperate struggle for survival. "There will always be poor people in the land, so I command you to give freely to your neighbors and to the poor and needy in your land" (Deuteronomy 15:11).

There are so many needy people that it's easy to feel overwhelmed—and to do nothing because we realize that we can't do everything. But God didn't ask us to do everything. He just asked us to do something.

NABAL

A Woman to the Rescue

Dumb as Nabal was, at least he had a smart wife: Abigail.

That's a tribute to the patriarchal system, which forced a woman to marry whomever her father told her to. Someone as smart as Abigail would never otherwise have chosen the likes of Nabal, described as "such a wicked man that no one can even talk to him" (1 Samuel 25:17).

One of Nabal's servants had the sense and the healthy survival instinct to go to Abigail and report Nabal's reckless behavior. "Terrible trouble is coming to our master and all his family," the servant told Abigail. "Now think about it, and decide what you can do."

Probably from food supplies prepared for the festival, Abigail gathered up:

- two hundred loaves of bread,
- two sheep-size leather bags full of wine,
- five butchered sheep,
- one hundred raisin cakes, and
- two hundred fig cakes (1 Samuel 25:18).

She loaded these on donkeys and set out toward David's camp. In what must have been a horrifying moment, she rode right into the army on its way to wipe out her entire family. Just before she came into sight, David had said: "It's been useless! I watched over Nabal's property in the desert. I made sure none of his sheep was missing. I did good to him, but he has paid me back with evil. . . . I will not leave one of Nabal's men alive until morning" (vv. 21–22).

Abigail quickly slid off her donkey and bowed on the ground before David. "My master," she said, "don't pay attention to this worthless man Nabal. He is like his name. His name means 'fool,' and he is truly a fool" (v. 25).

Abigail took the blame and asked for forgiveness for missing the men David sent earlier. Then she offered the gifts for his army and gave David a blessing, expressing hope that he would defeat his enemies and would one day become king of Israel. David accepted her gifts and told her to go home in peace. No one died that day.

Nabal, however, was in for a shock when he finally woke up from his drunken sleep the next day. Abigail told him everything, and "his heart stopped, and he became like stone. About ten days later the Lord struck Nabal and he died" (vv. 37–38).

The symptoms sound like a stroke, which can be brought on by high stress and can leave a person paralyzed "like stone."

God made great use of the dumb and now dead Nabal.

David married Abigail, and he assumed the property and prestige that had once belonged to Nabal. David's marriage to Abigail helps explain why he later carried so much influence in Hebron, located only about ten miles north of Nabal's home. It was in this key city in the tribal territory of Judah, Israel's biggest tribe, that the people of Judah later crowned David king. In time, Jews of other tribes rallied around David, confirming the decision of the Judeans.

David served his people with distinction, becoming the most revered king in Jewish history. That's thanks in no small part to the dumbness of a man named Fool.

Learning from Nabal's Mistake
God's Smart Use of Human Dumbness

God isn't limited by our stupidity. His character is love, and his mission is to save people from the harm that sin causes. Nothing is going to change either one of those. The Bible and our own experiences are full of the proof.

Nabal refused to give David's army supplies. But instead of threatening David's future, this actually worked to his advantage. David got everything.

Joseph's brothers, jealous of the special treatment he got from their father, sold him to slave traders. God saw to it that Joseph became the number two official in Egypt. When a seven-year drought hit Israel, Joseph saved his extended family by inviting them to graze their flocks by the Nile River. "You meant to hurt me," Joseph told his brothers, "but God turned your evil into good to save the lives of many people," (Genesis 50:20).

Two eighteen-year-old high school students I know of recently got married and moved in with the groom's parents two months before their baby was due. Christian neighbors have been reaching out to help the young couple. It's too early to tell what will become of this, but I believe it's very much in God's character to use this experience to draw the couple to faith in God and to allow the grandparents to develop a love for their grandson that will be deeper than they would ever have experienced had he been born years later in some distant city.

That's the kind of God we serve—wise enough to find some good in the bad and smart in the dumb.

No Question Is a Dumb Question

1. Do you think David was out of line by requesting supplies from Nabal for protecting his flocks, even though Nabal apparently didn't ask for the help? Was David justified in planning to kill Nabal for refusing, or was that an overreaction?

2. Why do you think Nabal thought he could get away with refusing to give supplies to an army? What could have possibly been his motivation for insulting David and his men?

3. The feature "How Much Is Enough?" refers to high salaries of sports figures and corporate executives. Why are their salaries so out of control? As Christians, do you think it's our responsibility to do something about that, or should we focus on the disparity between our income and that of the poor?

4. God made good use of Nabal's stupidity. When Nabal died, David married Nabal's wife and suddenly had much greater wealth and influence, which helped propel him to Israel's throne. What other examples can you think of from the Bible or from your experiences in life that show God's making good use of something bad or smart use of something dumb? What does that say about God?

5. In the feature "God's Smart Use of Human Dumbness," there's a reference to teenagers who get married because of pregnancy. How do you think Christians could help in a situation like that? What do you think some Christians might do that could be more harmful than helpful?

Nabal Recap

DUMB DECISIONS	ROTTEN RESULTS
He Insults David's soldiers and refuses to give them food, even though they protected his herds.	David assembles four hundred soldiers and rides out to kill Nabal.
He eats a feast and gets drunk, unaware that David's hungry soldiers are on their way.	Nabal's wife takes supplies to David, stopping the attack. When she tells Nabal what happened, he has some kind of attack of his own and dies. David gets everything by marrying Nabal's widow.

12
SAMSON

He could kill a lion with his bare hands,
but this muscleman morphed into a wimp around pretty women.

In the bountiful dumbness of Samson, there's one scene dumbest of all. He's napping with his head on Delilah's lap—and he expects to wake up with hair.

Normally, that would be a reasonable expectation for anyone falling asleep with someone they love. But Samson should have seen it coming. Three times he had lied to Delilah about how she could drain the strength right out of him. And three times she tried.

The fourth time, Samson told her the truth. And it never seemed to occur to him that she would try it again.

Delilah had compelling motivation: money. Bribed by Philistine leaders to discover the secret of Samson's incredible strength, she set out on a mission to nag Samson to death.

Nag 1. "Tell me why you are so strong. How can someone tie you up and capture you?" Delilah asked (Judges 16:6).

"Someone would have to tie me up with seven new bowstrings that have not been dried," Samson answered. "Then I would be as weak as any other man."

She tied him up. With seven new bowstrings. Then she hid some Philistines in the room. When she cried out that the Philistines had come to get him, he snapped the bowstrings (vv. 8–9).

Nag 2. "You made a fool of me," Delilah complained. "You lied to me. Now tell me how someone can tie you up."

"They would have to tie me with new ropes that have not been used before. Then I would become as weak as any other man."

She tied him up. With new ropes. When she called in the soldiers, Samson popped off the ropes (vv. 10–12).

Nag 3. "Again you have made a fool of me. You lied to me. Tell me how someone can tie you up."

"Using the loom," Samson said, "weave the seven braids of my hair into the cloth, and tighten it with a pin. Then I will be as weak as any other man."

After a nap, Samson woke up with a weave in his hair, and his hair in a loom. But he was as strong as ever (vv. 13–14).

Nag 4. "How can you say, 'I love you,' when you don't even trust me? This is the third time you have made a fool of me. You haven't told me the secret of your great strength" (v. 15).

Anyone with cerebral neurons firing on all synapses would have answered something like this: "Why should I confide in you? Three times I told you how to hurt me, and three times you tried."

Samson, however, told her exactly what she wanted to hear. "I have never had my hair cut. . . . If someone shaved my head, I would lose my strength and be as weak as any other man" (v. 17).

Sometimes love makes people do stupid things. So does relentless nagging.

Even then, it's hard to understand why Samson would fall asleep with his hairy head on Delilah's lap and expect to wake up with anything other than a buzz.

It's an odd coincidence that Samson's name means "little sun," as in the nickname Sunny Boy. It's odd because Delilah's name sounds a lot like the Hebrew word for night: *layla.* She turned the lights out on Samson.

Learning from Samson's Mistake
People Who Pitch a Fit

Constant pestering can wear us down, especially if it comes from someone we care about—and even more so if they get all worked up. Yelling, crying, and spitting out accusations designed to impose guilt can break us down all the faster, compelling us to give in to the wishes of another, against our better judgment.

Whether it's in a committee meeting at work or during a family argument in the living room, people pitching a fit to get their own way are little more than terrorists trying to hold us hostage and manipulate us with their emotions.

We shouldn't make our decision just to get those folks calmed down and off our back. If they're upset, it's their problem. We can't control how others react to decisions we make that are in our best interest. But if we let their emotions manipulate us into making a bad decision, then it's our problem. Think of it that way. They've got a problem, and they would rather we have a problem.

Delilah wanted money, but she needed Samson's secret. That was her problem. It wasn't Samson's problem at all—not until he told her his secret. Then suddenly he had a big problem all his own.

Samson learned the hard way, but we don't have to.

THE DUMBNESS BEGINS

Though Samson's haircut was probably the dumbest thing he brought on himself, he filled his life with bad choices that spawned tragic results. And every bad choice started with his weakness for unsavory women.

What's so surprising about Samson is that when we read the beginning of his story, we expect more of him.

He was a miracle baby, born to a Hebrew couple who hadn't

been able to conceive: Manoah and his unidentified wife. That put Samson in the company of some of Israel's most distinguished leaders: Isaac, Joseph, Samuel, and John the Baptist. An angel told Samson's mother that her son would distinguish himself too: "You must never cut his hair, because he will be a Nazirite, given to God from birth. He will begin to save Israel from the power of the Philistines" (Judges 13:5).

As a lifetime Nazirite, Samson was supposed to obey three main rules:

- Don't eat grapes or drink wine made from them.
- Don't go near anything dead.
- Don't cut your hair.

One by one, he broke all three rules. He started by eating honey from the carcass of a lion. Then at his wedding, wine flowed freely. The haircut came later.

Samson also broke a basic law that all Israelites were to follow: he married a non-Israelite. God had warned his people against this: "Do not marry any of them.... If you do, those people will turn your children away from me, to begin serving other gods" (Deuteronomy 7:3–4).

When Samson told his parents that he intended to marry a Philistine in the neighboring village, their jaws dropped. "Surely there is a woman from Israel you can marry," they said. "Do you have to marry a woman from the Philistines, who are not circumcised?" (Judges 14:3).

Reason lost.

Religion lost.

Hormones won. So began Samson's lifetime of dumb decisions.

THE WEDDING MURDERS

Samson's sad tale actually starts with a pair of dumb decisions: eating the carcass honey and marrying a Philistine honey, an unidentified woman he met before Delilah. Both produced horrifying results at his weeklong wedding celebration.

The carcass honey found its way into a riddle: "Out of the eater comes something to eat. Out of the strong comes something sweet" (Judges 14:14).

Samson bet his thirty Philistine guests they couldn't solve this riddle. If they did, he would give them each a set of clothes. If they didn't, they each owed him a set of clothes.

Wedding celebrations typically lasted a week. Four days into the party, the guests were getting worried they'd lose their bet—so worried that they pulled the bride aside. They told her to get the answer for them if she didn't want her father's house burned down with her in it.

Years before Delilah nagged Samson to death, this unidentified Philistine bride used some of the same techniques, with equal success.

"You hate me! You don't really love me!" she cried. "You told my people a riddle, but you won't tell me the answer" (v. 16).

In a surprising show of wisdom, Samson refused. For three days. But on day seven of the celebration, his bride's nagging got the best of him.

Samson told her the answer. She told the guests. And the guests repeated it back to Samson. "What is sweeter than honey? What is stronger than a lion?" (v. 18).

Furious at his guests as well as his bride, Samson charged off to a neighboring city a day's walk away. There, he killed thirty Philistine men, stole their clothes, and paid off his debt. Then he stormed home to his mother and father, abandoning his wife.

By the time he calmed down and returned to his bride, she had married the best man. "I thought you really hated your wife," the bride's father explained. "So I gave her to your best man. Her younger sister is more beautiful. Take her instead" (Judges 15:2).

Samson's temper lit up like the Philistine countryside he soon set on fire. "This time no one will blame me for hurting you Philistines," he warned his ex-father-in-law (v. 3).

Learning from Samson's Mistake
Break a Rule, Hurt Yourself

We don't have to live by some of the laws God gave Samson; those were unique to him. But we have our own God-given laws, and we know what they are. The basics are in the Ten Commandments with laws such as don't lie, don't steal, and don't commit adultery.

If we break one of God's laws, and do something we know is wrong, we might as well break our own arm. We hurt ourselves when we break God's rules. Those rules are there to protect us. It's like telling children not to touch the hot stove. Too often, curiosity wins and their fingers lose.

The stakes are often higher for adults. Our curiosity, passion, or greed can win, but it can cost us jobs, relationships, and our reputation.

PHILISTINES ON FIRE

Samson caught three hundred foxes, tied them by their tails in pairs, and then lashed flaming torches to their tails. That assured the animals would run at top speed—perhaps in a zigzag as they tried to separate, laying down a wide trail of arson.

There was plenty to burn since it was springtime, and the

Philistines lived in a rich coastal pasture. Ripe grain waved in the fields, and vineyards and olive orchards grew their fruit.

Samson's fire took out:

- grain fields as well as grain stored in bundles—a year's crop lost.
- vineyards—three to five years of crops lost. That's how long it took newly planted vines to grow grapes.
- olive groves—a generation of crops lost. Without modern farming techniques, it took olive trees forty to fifty years to become fully productive. Farmers who planted olive trees were planting them for their grandchildren.

Samson thought the fire was a good idea—a just idea. He was wrong. Once Philistine leaders found out that Samson started the fire because of what his bride and her father did, they burned both daughter and dad to death. Middle East justice: eye for eye, tooth for tooth, fire for fire.

In Samson's sequel of bad ideas, he declared a one-man guerrilla war on the Philistines. He killed many before retreating to a cave in the Judean hills in what is now southern Israel. But the Philistine army followed, invading Israel and taking one town hostage. A force of three thousand Israelites went after Samson and pleaded with him to give himself up so the Philistines would leave them in peace. Samson agreed, but once the Philistines took him into custody, he snapped the rope that bound him and slaughtered a thousand Philistine soldiers with a donkey's jawbone. Brains and lofty ideals had nothing to do with Samson's drive. It was lowbrow instinct—a lust for revenge and women.

The next time he shows up, he's visiting a Philistine prostitute. After that, comes his fatal attraction, Delilah, who delivers him head-shaved to the Philistines for twenty-eight pounds of silver from each of five Philistine leaders—one hundred forty pounds total. That was probably more than her own weight in silver. With that money, she could have bought more than one hundred eighty slaves at the price set in Exodus 21:32.

Even Samson's last words, a prayer, were selfish. Paraded in front of a Philistine crowd assembled in a temple, blind Samson prayed, "God, please give me strength one more time so I can pay these Philistines back for putting out my two eyes!" (Judges 16:28).

He pushed on support pillars, which were typically blocks of wood or stone mounted on top of each other. The building collapsed, and Samson died with thousands of Philistines—more than all those he had killed before.

Learning from Samson's Mistake
Getting Even

It seems like the natural thing to do. Someone hurts us, and we give them a taste of their own medicine. Some folks even argue that it's the biblical thing to do: an eye for an eye and a tooth for a tooth. But that was a common law throughout the ancient Middle East, an attempt to administer justice in the courts. It wasn't God's blessing on revenge.

Retaliation produces retaliation, which produces more retaliation. That has been nowhere more obvious than in modern Israel. A Palestinian wanting his homeland back blows up Israeli civilians on a bus. The Israeli government blows up the homes of the bomber and his relatives or launches a missile attack into Palestinian territory. Generations of retaliation has produced unimaginable hate.

It works the same way in our private lives. Retaliation produces retaliation. Hate grows and takes over, leaving no room for reconciliation.

The only way the cycle of retaliation ends is when someone decides not to get even. They decide to stay odd and to turn the other cheek. Nothing seems odder, until we witness for ourselves the power that forgiveness has to heal the hurt and restore the relationship.

PUTTING DUMB DECISIONS TO GOOD USE

The Bible doesn't say God programmed Samson for dumbness. But it does say God put the dumbness to good use.

Before Samson came along, Philistines and Israelites lived in peace, exchanging in trade and marrying each other. Since Philistines were the stronger nation, the Israelites were in danger of becoming assimilated—of losing their unique identity.

Samson drove a wedge between the two, turning them suspicious of each other. What Samson started, King David finished about fifty years later—defeating and dismantling the Philistine army.

In time, Philistines vanished from history, assimilated into other Middle Eastern nations. All that's left of them is the Greek form of their name: Palestine.

NO QUESTION IS A DUMB QUESTION

1. Why do you think Samson fell asleep on Delilah's lap and expected to wake up with hair, given the fact that she had already tried to take away his strength three times? Was it a testimonial to the power of Delilah's nagging, to Samson's wishful thinking, or to something else—perhaps a very large wineskin?

2. We've all seen people who get their way through constant pestering. How have you seen it work? How can we fight back and win? Does it help to think of the pestering person as a terrorist who is trying to hold us hostage with his or her emotions? Or is it better to think of the person as having a problem that they he or she is trying to shift to us?

3. "Break a Rule, Hurt Yourself" says that God's laws are there to protect us. Why do we often treat God's laws as if they're intended to keep us from having fun? What kind of injuries have you seen from people ignoring God's laws?

4. In the fight between Samson and the Philistines, violence met with retaliation which met with more violence—a continuing cycle. How have you seen the same thing in the world today or perhaps among people you know? What does it take to break the cycle? Have you ever witnessed something like this?

5. God put Samson's dumb decisions to good use, driving a wedge between Philistines and Israelites. How have you seen God turn dumbness around, using it for good?

Samson Recap

DUMB DECISIONS	ROTTEN RESULTS
He marries a Philistine.	The marriage doesn't last a week.
He abandons his wife for helping cheat him.	She marries the best man.
He burns Philistine farms in retaliation.	Philistines burn his ex-wife.
He tells Delilah his strength is in his hair.	She gives him a haircut. Then she turns him over to Philistines, who blind and imprison him.
He prays for revenge and manages to collapse a crowded Philistine temple.	He's in the temple at the time. He dies.

13

SOLOMON

Internationally famous for his wisdom,
this king of Israel aged into an old, idol worshiping fool.

Wisest man in human history, Solomon did the dumbest thing of all.

Dumber than a donkey herder, he did what Saul, who left his herd to become Israel's first king, would have considered too risky.

And dumber than his dad, he did what King David, who impregnated a married woman when he already had half a dozen wives, would have considered reckless.

Solomon broke God's first law—the most important law. The law that when broken sucks the life out of all other laws, leaving them dead and useless. "You must not have any other gods except me" (Exodus 20:3).

Not only did Solomon worship other gods, but he chose two of the most despicable. People worshiped these two gods with sex rituals and human sacrifice. Following Solomon's lead, Jews would continue worshiping them for four hundred years until God finally wiped their nation off the map, like cleaning a dirt spot on a carpet.

We expected more of Solomon, and with good reason. He was probably still in his twenties when he became Israel's third king, and when God made him a startling promise like none other in all of the Bible: "I will give you wisdom and understanding that is greater than anyone has had in the past or will have in the future" (1 Kings 3:12).

But wisdom, it seems, is no match for stupidity.

BEFORE THE DUMBNESS

Tenth son of King David, Solomon was a long shot to become king. The throne usually went to the oldest son. This time, however, David selected the son of his favorite wife, Bathsheba, to succeed him.

That came as a shock to David's oldest son, Adonijah, who was throwing himself a precoronation party while his father lay dying. Yet that callous revelry must have helped confirm for David that he had made the right choice. When David heard about the party, he instructed the high priest and prophet Nathan to declare Solomon king, to honor the promise he had made to Bathsheba.

David's deathbed declaration seems one of the smartest of his life, because Solomon started his reign by asking for God's help. He traveled to the most important Jewish worship center at the time, at Gibeon about seven miles north of Jerusalem. And there he made a sacrifice so lavish that some Bible experts wonder if the writer was exaggerating: a thousand burnt offerings.

Solomon spent the night at Gibeon, and God came to him in a dream. "Ask for whatever you want me to give you," God said.

"LORD my God, now you have made me, your servant, king in my father's place. But I am like a little child; I don't know how to do what must be done. I, your servant, am here among your chosen people, and there are too many of them to count. I ask that you give me an obedient heart so I can rule the people in the right way and will know the difference between right and wrong. Otherwise, it is impossible to rule this great people of yours" (1 Kings 3:7–9).

God was impressed and promised to give him not only the wisdom he asked for but wealth and honor as well. "During your life no other king will be as great as you," God replied (v. 13).

SOLOMON'S SPLIT DECISION

The very next scene in Solomon's story offers powerful evidence that he got his wish. He had to settle a dispute between two prostitutes who delivered sons about the same time and who lived together. One woman rolled onto her baby in the night, accidentally killing him. When she discovered what had happened, she swapped babies while her roommate was still sleeping.

Solomon's method of determining the real mother of the breathing baby was as effective as a DNA test. But instead of looking for blood links, he looked for love links. He sent his servants to get a sword, and then ordered them to "Cut the living baby into two pieces, and give each woman half" (1 Kings 3:25).

People reading the story today may think that sounds like an obvious trick and that the women should have known Solomon would do nothing of the kind. But ancient Middle Eastern rulers had a long history of violent behavior. One Egyptian king ordered the nose cut off anyone interfering with boat traffic on the Nile. Assyrian rulers cut off noses too—along with ears and lips. The Bible tells of a king in what is now Jordan poking out the right eye of every Israelite he could find. Kings with sharp instruments were considered unpredictably dangerous.

The kidnapper sided with her judge: "Neither of us will have him. Cut him into two pieces!"

"Please," the real mother said to Solomon, "don't kill him! Give the baby to her!" (v. 26). Love link established, Solomon gave the real mother her boy.

Word of this court case spread quickly, and the citizens of

Israel grew to respect Solomon and to value the wisdom that God had so obviously given him.

PRICE TAG FOR A GOLDEN AGE

David had set Israel on the path to a golden age by defeating the neighboring enemies. And Solomon took Israel the rest of the way home, ruling them forty years during an unprecedented time of peace and prosperity. With no major battles to fight, he could build to his heart's content—and to the nation's discontent.

Decades earlier, when the Jews demanded a king so they could be like other nations, the prophet Samuel warned them what was coming. "If you have a king ruling over you, this is what he will do:

- Take your sons and make them serve with his chariots and his horses, and they will run in front of the king's chariot....
- Make some of your other sons plow his ground and reap his harvest. He will take others to make weapons of war and equipment for his chariots....
- Take your daughters to make perfume and cook and bake for him....
- Take your best fields, vineyards, and olive groves and give them to his servants....
- Take one-tenth of your grain and grapes and give it to his officers and servants....
- Take your male and female servants, your best cattle, and your donkeys and use them all for his own work....
- Take one-tenth of your flocks, and you yourselves will become his slaves."

"When that time comes," Samuel added, "you will cry out because of the king you chose" (1 Samuel 8:11–18).

With Solomon's coronation, that time had come. And Samuel's

more-than-a-wish list proved to be just page one of Solomon's blueprint for a golden age. He took on the staggering and expensive job of building, rebuilding, and fortifying cities all over the country—at least sixteen of them.

He built Israel's first temple—a dazzling, cut-stone, gold-paneled shrine that took one hundred eighty thousand drafted workers seven years to build. Grunts included thirty thousand Israelites forced to work on one of three lumberjack crews of ten thousand men each—one month on, two months off. They cut rot-resistant cedar trees in Lebanon, and then floated the logs down the seacoast and dragged them over the Judean hills. Eighty thousand other men worked in quarries as stone cutters. Another seventy thousand hauled the cut stones up to the Jerusalem hilltop where the temple was rising.

An even bigger project was his sprawling palace, the House of the Forest of Lebanon. It took nearly twice as long to build as the temple—thirteen years—and who knows how much forced labor. The Bible doesn't say.

The price tag for all of this was astronomical, not only in terms of Israelites ordered away from their farms and herds to work for the king but in land traded away as well. Solomon gave twenty Galilean cities to his neighbor in the north, the king of Tyre in what is now Lebanon, to help pay him for wood and gold he supplied. That's a bit like the American president giving Washington State to Canada in exchange for some of that fine Vancouver timber.

Solomon had other needs as well. Just to feed his family and palace officials, each day the Bible says he needed:

- 195 bushels of fine flour,
- 390 bushels of grain,
- ten cows fed on good grain,
- twenty cows raised in the fields,

- one hundred sheep,
- three kinds of deer and gazelles, and
- a flock of fattened birds (1 Kings 4:22–23).

To help pay for his splendor, he collected tolls from caravans traveling on the international trade routes he controlled—and he controlled all of the land routes connecting Africa and Arabia in the south to Middle Eastern nations in the north. In addition, he forced less powerful nations to pay him taxes. He also did some lucrative trading of his own. In a joint trading venture with the seafaring nation of Tyre, he operated a fleet of ships in the Red Sea.

Among his own people, he established a strong central government by dismantling the centuries-old system of twelve tribes and replacing it with twelve districts—a bit like states—run by appointed governors. These districts ignored tribal boundaries, which probably angered a lot of his people. But the new structure shifted more power to him, making it easier to run the nation and collect taxes to pay the staggering bills.

Learning from Solomon's Mistake
Running to the Wrong Goal

Sometimes we want something so badly that we'll do just about anything to get it. We set the goal, and the goal becomes our god. We devote ourselves to it. We obsess about it. We go to war over it.

It might be a job promotion, a love interest, a nest egg, a bigger house, or a flashy chariot pulled by two hundred horses.

To reach that goal, we cast our eyes like steel on the then and there, blind to the here and now. In the garden at our feet, we trample flowers—our children, spouse, friends, and co-workers. Anyone between us and our goal.

God didn't tell Solomon to build a glorious kingdom at any cost. He doesn't tell us to do that either. In one concise statement, Jesus summed up the goal above all goals: "One must love God with all his heart, all his mind, and all his strength. And one must love his neighbor as he loves himself" (Mark 12:33).

It's fine to have goals, to look ahead, and to set our sights high. But not if it turns us from God or stamps our footprints on fragile souls.

THE MARRYING KIND

Marriage between one man and one woman is hard enough to survive, religion intact. Solomon married a thousand—seven hundred women of royal birth and three hundred secondary wives.

His religion didn't have a prayer.

Wisest guy on earth, he probably thought he was doing the smart thing. He married royalty from most if not all of his neighboring nations and trading partners. It was a custom of the time for nations to seal their deals with a kiss—a marriage between two royal families. It seemed to help ensure the peace. The king of Egypt, for example, would think twice about attacking or cheating Solomon if a princess of Egypt lived in the Jerusalem harem. This seemed to make plenty of sense, given the nervous political climate.

But Jews who remembered their religious law and history knew it was dumber than a honeymoon in Sodom.

A few hundred years earlier, Moses had given the Jews this warning about the locals: "Do not marry any of them, or let your daughters marry their sons, or let your sons marry their daughters. If you do, those people will turn your children away from me, to begin serving other gods. Then the LORD will be very angry with you, and he will quickly destroy you. This is what you must do to those people: Tear down their altars, smash their holy stone pillars, cut down their Asherah idols, and burn their idols in the fire" (Deuteronomy 7:3 5).

Solomon did exactly the opposite. He married the forbidden women. And in his old age he built up what he should have been tearing down. "On a hill east of Jerusalem, Solomon built two places for worship. One was a place to worship Chemosh, the hated god of the Moabites, and the other was a place to worship Molech, the hated god of the Ammonites. Solomon did the same thing for all his foreign wives so they could burn incense and offer sacrifices to their gods" (1 Kings 11:7–8).

Solomon joined in the worship. How he worshiped is unknown. But at least two later kings who descended from him, Ahaz and Manasseh, sacrificed their sons. People had been sacrificing their children to Molech centuries before Solomon. That's clear because Moses had warned the Israelites, "You must not give any of your children to be sacrificed to Molech" (Leviticus 18:21).

For Solomon's disobedience, God vowed, "I will tear your kingdom away from you and give it to one of your officers. . . . I will tear it away from your son when he becomes king. . . . but I will leave him one tribe to rule" (1 Kings 11:11–13).

Learning from Solomon's Mistake
Nibbling Our Way into Trouble

We human beings tend to get in trouble the way sheep do. We don't go looking for a dead-end ledge on a mountain cliff. We nibble our way there.

Solomon probably had no intention of worshiping idols. He may not even have realized he was breaking God's law by marrying foreign women who could lure him into their pagan worship rituals. But for Solomon, one thing led to another.

It works the same way with us. The Bible and the Holy Spirit alert us to critical boundary markers. When we walk right past them, we're heading into a danger zone and away from our only reliable source of help.

When we lie, we put ourselves at risk by building a web that will one day snag us. When we steal, we ratchet up the odds of finding ourselves on the receiving end of smash-mouth retaliation. And when we flirt with someone else's spouse, we flirt with trouble that can devastate more lives than we can tally with a calculator.

The boundaries are there not to restrict us but to protect us, to let us know when danger is ahead. The dumb thing to do is nibble on past them.

DIVIDED THEY FALL

By the time Solomon died, Israel had endured forty years of all the peace and glory they cared to pay for in high taxes and elbow grease. They wanted a change. So they asked for it.

Solomon's son, however, promised more of the same—and then some. "My father forced you to work hard, but I will make you work even harder. My father beat you with whips, but I will beat you with whips that have sharp points" (1 Kings 12:14). All the northern Jewish tribes walked, leaving the king to rule his own tribe of Judah.

The northern tribes crowned as king one of Solomon's previous foremen, Jeroboam. He had run off to Egypt to get away from Solomon, and he didn't come back until the king died. This northern Jewish nation became known as Israel, while the smaller Jewish nation that remained loyal to Solomon's son took the name of the royal family's tribe: Judah.

But Jeroboam was a big dummy too. He set up golden bull shrines for the people to worship. This northern nation of Israel survived another two hundred years before Assyrian invaders scrapped it off the world map and then exiled the survivors. Judah lasted about another one hundred fifty years after that, until Babylonian invaders leveled the towns and exiled the survivors.

The land that God had promised to the Jews "forever" was no longer theirs. That's because of an "if" clause.

"If you do not obey me and keep all my commands, and if you turn away from my rules and hate my laws, refusing to obey all my commands, you have broken our agreement.... I will destroy your places where gods are worshiped and cut down your incense altars. I will pile your dead bodies on the lifeless forms of your idols.... I will scatter you among the nations, and I will pull out my sword and destroy you. Your land will become empty, your cities a waste" (Leviticus 26:14–15; 30–33).

The wisest man in the world turned his people away from God. And the people followed—all the way to the dead end.

NO QUESTION IS A DUMB QUESTION

1. Why is it shocking to see Solomon in a book called *Big Dummies of the Bible*? If we had to create a Top Ten list of things for which Solomon is famous, what would some of them be?

2. Take a look at the warnings Samuel gave about kings, the nasty things kings would demand of the people (page 144). What do you think would have been hardest for the citizens to put up with?

3. Do you think Solomon's goal of a grand kingdom was a good one? Or was it a flawed goal because it required him to stamp his "footprints on fragile souls"? What over-the-top goals do people today often seek, no matter what it costs? What is often the cost?

4. What kind of influence does the faith of one spouse typically have on the other? What have you noticed about couples who don't share the same faith?

5. Solomon seemed to nibble his way into trouble, a little bit at a time—or maybe a wife at a time. How do we nibble our way into trouble? What are some boundary markers that are intended to alert us to trouble ahead?

Solomon Recap

DUMB DECISIONS	ROTTEN RESULTS
He marries women from other nations and worships their idols.	God vows to tear away most of the kingdom from his family.
He oppresses citizens by overtaxing them and drafting them for massive building projects.	The nation splits in two— north and south.

A free leader's guide

for groups using

Big Dummies of the Bible

is available at the

author's Web site:

www.stephenmiller.info